THE PUBLIC SERVANT'S GUIDE TO GOVERNMENT IN CANADA

THE PUBLIC SERVANT'S GUIDE TO GOVERNMENT IN CANADA

Alex Marland and Jared J. Wesley

UNIVERSITY OF TORONTO PRESS

Toronto Buffalo London

Library and Archives Canada Cataloguing in Publication

Marland, Alexander J., 1973–, author
The public servant's guide to government in Canada / Alex Marland and Jared J. Wesley.

Includes bibliographical references and index.
Issued in print and electronic formats.

ISBN 978-1-4875-9476-3 (softcover). ISBN 978-1-4875-9477-0 (hardcover).
ISBN 978-1-4875-9478-7 (epub). ISBN 978-1-4875-9479-4 (uPDF).

    1. Civil service – Canada. 2. Civil service – Canada – Handbooks, manuals, etc.
3. Public administration – Canada. 4. Public administration – Canada – Handbooks,
manuals, etc. 5. Civil service positions – Canada. I. Wesley, Jared J., 1980–, author II. Title.

JL108.M368 2019   352.6′30971   C2018-902955-2
                                                                                           C2018-902956-0

We welcome comments and suggestions regarding any aspect of our publications—
please feel free to contact us at news@utorontopress.com or visit our Internet site at
utorontopress.com.

North America
5201 Dufferin Street
North York, Ontario, Canada, M3H 5T8

2250 Military Road
Tonawanda, New York, USA, 14150

ORDERS PHONE: 1–800–565–9523
ORDERS FAX: 1–800–221–9985
ORDERS E-MAIL: utpbooks@utpress.utoronto.ca

UK, Ireland, and continental Europe
NBN International
Estover Road, Plymouth, PL6 7PY, UK

ORDERS PHONE: 44 (0) 1752 202301
ORDERS FAX: 44 (0) 1752 202333
ORDERS E-MAIL: enquiries@nbninternational.com

Every effort has been made to contact copyright holders; in the event of an error or
omission, please notify the publisher.

This book is printed on paper containing 100% post-consumer fibre.

University of Toronto Press acknowledges the financial assistance to its publishing
program of the Canada Council for the Arts and the Ontario Arts Council, an agency of
the Government of Ontario.

 Canada Council for the Arts   **Conseil des Arts du Canada**   

Funded by the Government of Canada   Financé par le gouvernement du Canada   

CONTENTS

FIGURES AND TABLES

ACKNOWLEDGEMENTS

Many reviewers provided feedback to improve the contents of this book, ranging from conceptual comments to practical advice. We appreciate the detailed input provided to the University of Toronto Press from two anonymous referees. In addition, we collected tips and feedback from current and former public servants and political personnel. Alex Marland wishes to acknowledge the Hon. Edward Roberts, a former lieutenant governor and cabinet minister in Newfoundland and Labrador; Robert Thompson, a former clerk of the executive council and deputy minister in the Government of Newfoundland and Labrador; Stephanie Roy, a political staffer in the Government of Manitoba; Christel Binnie, a federal public servant in Ottawa; Clifford Grinling, a former public servant in Newfoundland and Labrador; and Bachelor of Commerce students Jessi Drohan and Yichen Fan, who completed co-operative education placements with the Government of Canada. Jared Wesley thanks David Morhart, who has served as president of the Institute of Public Administration of Canada and in various deputy minister and executive management roles in Alberta and British Columbia; Carolyn Campbell, deputy city manager at the City of Edmonton and former deputy minister with the Government of Alberta; Mike Phillips, who has held various analyst and advisor roles with the Government of Alberta; and Carolina Calderon, a federal public servant and manager with Western Economic Diversification Canada. The authors also appreciate the input received from some public servants, political staffers, and students who wish to remain anonymous. These reviewers' willingness to help exemplifies their commitment to public service, though it does not necessarily constitute endorsement of the final content. We welcome further suggestions from readers.

PURPOSE OF *THE PUBLIC SERVANT'S GUIDE TO GOVERNMENT IN CANADA*

Chances are you have begun a career in government or aspire to do so. It is a noble and challenging profession. As this guide explains, public servants are expected to be loyal, skilled, dependable, and, above all, professional. They work in concert with the appointed members of cabinet and their political staff, who oversee the government and whose tenure tends to be much shorter. This guide encompasses all of these types of positions, but will be of greatest value to co-operative education students, early career professionals, and anyone who is new to the nonpartisan public service. It is designed for people who have limited awareness of the role and operations of government institutions, how public policy is developed and implemented, and how public servants interact with managers and political staff.

You should read this book:

- if you are interested in learning about how public administration works in practice and how to navigate the public service;
- if you want to move up the organizational ladder in government by learning about where you fit in the public service and how you can achieve your career goals; and
- regardless of whether you have taken courses in Canadian political science, in public administration, or in public policy.

The Public Servant's Guide to Government in Canada is an overview and introduction to life in the public service. It connects theory and practice to produce a handy desk reference. It contains practical advice for seeking a government job (see box below), building your career, self-assessing your competencies, and seeking assistance with improving your skill sets. It offers background information that new public servants need to know to make sense of where they work and the power relations they will experience.

Tips for Finding Your First Government Job

People often struggle to land their first government position. Here are some things to keep in mind. First, the public sector is enormous. Don't limit yourself to federal and provincial job sites; many municipalities, Indigenous organizations, and agencies, boards, and commissions have separate job boards. When you apply, tailor your application. Hiring managers have little difficulty discerning applicants who want any job from those who want their specific job; place yourself in the latter category by demonstrating the desire and capability to fill the position. Next, emphasize your related work and volunteer experience. Employers care surprisingly little about your credentials, grades, or research. Remember: you are competing with dozens or even hundreds of applicants with post-secondary qualifications. To distinguish yourself, emphasize the skills and knowledge acquired through experience. The use of competency keywords, discussed in **Chapter 6,** will help. Lastly, be patient and perseverant. Even the most talented people fail to be screened into interviews and don't receive job offers. Decisions in tight competitions come down to how well the various applicants would fit into the team dynamic of the organization. Much of this is beyond your control. Maintaining focus on your purpose and building your competencies to fit the job market will help you remain resilient.[1]

In short, *The Public Servant's Guide to Government in Canada* seeks to prepare you for a career in government. Employment opportunities are appearing as baby boomers retire. Globalization, technological innovation, shifting demographics, demands for accountability and results, and evolving workplace expectations are among the many changes that the public service is confronting.[2] A more diverse, interconnected workforce is emerging. This book aims to prepare you for the opportunities and challenges that await.

Notes

1   For more advice, see Wesley (2017).
2   Privy Council Office (2013).

Tips Wanted!

Have suggestions for how this concise book can be improved? We'd like to hear them! Look up Alex Marland and/or Jared Wesley online and send us an email with your tip(s). With your permission we might incorporate your ideas into a future edition. We look forward to learning from you.

CHAPTER 1

REVIEW OF CORE CONCEPTS

The authors recognize that readers have different backgrounds, training, experience, and information needs. You are encouraged to peruse the chapters and content that you believe to be most applicable to your situation at a given time. Some readers may find it helpful to consult the Glossary of Terms on page 97.

Public servants make choices and take actions that profoundly shape Canadians' lives every day. Our homes are safer because of the building code standards they help develop and enforce. The food we eat and the medicines we use are of higher quality and potentially lower cost because public servants provide oversight. Internet, radio, television, and print media content that we consume is influenced by policies they administer. Public servants play a role in developing and implementing all public policy related to our cars, the roads we travel, speed limits, the price of gasoline and insurance, who is licensed to drive, the availability of public transportation, whether there are bike lanes, and the rules of the road. In fact, by the time most Canadians arrive at their destination to begin the workday, chances are they will have indirectly interacted with government hundreds of times. Some may go on to have direct interactions during their day. Perhaps they will visit a government website, contact a politician, visit a hospital clinic, pay a tax bill, or argue over a parking ticket. We all regularly engage with various forms of government and, by extension, with the employees who loyally implement the policy decisions made by those holding political office.

In many ways, public servants stand on the front lines of Canadian democracy. Whether offering policy advice to cabinet ministers, delivering services to citizens, or working in concert with political staff, their roles require familiarity with common principles that underpin the practice of politics and governance in Canada. A refresher for some and a primer for others, this chapter summarizes core concepts about democratic governance and public administration.

What Is a Public Servant?

Generally speaking, we are concerned with the nonpartisan workers in the core public service, namely those in government departments, Crown corporations, and agencies. They are alternatively known as civil servants and bureaucrats, but for consistency we refer to them as public servants. This encompasses the permanent, salaried personnel in government and those on contracts, including short-term staff such as interns and co-operative education students. The roles and responsibilities of these employees are the focus of *The Public Servant's Guide to Government in Canada*.

Working in government can be a demanding and rewarding career path, one that directly employs roughly 4 million Canadians,[1] as part of the world's most effective civil service.[2] Examples of the thousands of public servant job titles include:

- airport response specialist
- area licensing administrator
- bilingual branch library technician
- chief cook on a marine vessel
- citizen services officer
- community social service worker
- competition law officer
- director of integration and multiculturalism
- economic development analyst
- environmental planner
- equipment operator
- junior program analyst
- laboratory manager
- manager, strategic planning
- program coordinator
- public outreach education officer

This book emphasizes the roles and duties of public servants in the federal and provincial governments of Canada. Some content applies to employees in territorial, municipal, and Indigenous governments. Politicians and political staff are featured throughout this book because they work closely with public servants. Other people on the public payroll are not strictly considered public servants because government is not their primary employer. Public sector workers such as teachers, nurses, doctors, professors, military personnel, police and corrections officers, and others are subject to their own professional codes. They have their own separate training facilities, regulatory bodies, associations, and unions. What all of them have in common is that public sector workers are paid, at least in part, using public money. Moreover they are all subject to decisions made by the small number of decision-makers who run the government.

Core Principles of Canadian Government

Democratic government is messy and confusing.[3] *Democracy* means that the authority of those who govern is derived from the people being governed. But all citizens cannot be satisfied all the time. Some may go as far as to challenge the legitimacy or mandate of those overseeing the government, especially if the ruling party failed to receive a majority of votes in the previous election. What is more, politicians must juggle short-term pressures and long-term implications. They are motivated by competing ideologies and agendas. The interests of the majority push up against minority rights—even the very system of electing representatives is subject to debate. So anyone engaged with Canadian politics and government should understand that criticism is inevitable. In fact, citizens publicly complaining and demanding change is a hallmark of a free society. The extent to which government personnel are aware, concerned about, and positioned to respond to those demands adds another layer of complexity.

In a democracy there is a constant struggle for public resources and lobbying for political decisions to favour some individuals and groups. A general election is a peaceful way to sort out political conflict. Voters come together at polling booths to determine which politicians should represent them, ultimately form a cabinet to oversee the government, and implement campaign promises. Voting involves trade-offs: we might like only certain aspects of a party's election platform, for instance. Some voters simply place their trust in a given party label, a leader, or local candidate to do what's best.

Tip: Most Canadians Don't Follow Government Activities
Public servants should bear in mind that many, if not most, citizens do not pay much attention to politics or public policy.

The competition of ideas persists post-election. We hear about some politicking, such as protests by organized interests and activists that attract news coverage. Much we don't, such as private meetings among politicians and the representatives of businesses, labour unions, and other organized interests. Politicians weigh all available information as they seek to advance a political agenda and shape the norms, practices, decisions, and rules of government. Collectively, those outcomes are known as *public policy*.

There are a number of phases in public policy, discussed in greater detail in **Chapter 3**. Ideas attract public attention, are debated, developed, implemented, and evaluated. At each phase, public servants and political staff perform various interdependent functions. This process of *public administration* is not itself a democracy. It is not up to public servants to decide policy; that is the role of ministers who are accountable to the legislature and the public. As well, higher ranking public servants have more say than those of a lower rank. Given these realities, public servants must follow what is known as the *public service bargain*, discussed in **Chapter 2**. They should provide fearless advice to their superiors and political masters and, when a political decision is made, loyally implement that decision within the bounds of the law and the constitution. Public servants must therefore never let their personal views interfere with their ability to follow a chain of command. A functional bureaucracy depends on an efficient organizational hierarchy (Figure 1). Staff must follow the lawful directives of those who hold decision-making authority, including elected and non-elected senior officials. This helps ensure that employees throughout the public service are always acting on behalf

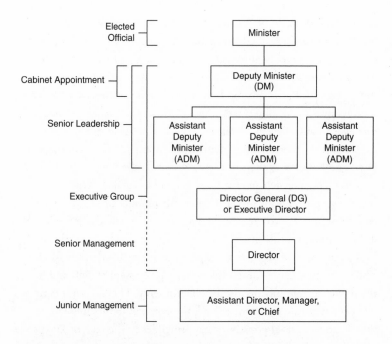

FIGURE 1 Senior Hierarchy in a Government Department

Note: Ministers do not have to be elected officials. DMs are appointed through an Order in Council, which is normally requested by the first minister and not subject to cabinet discussion. Source: Adapted from Government of Canada, "Canadian Federal Government Departmental Senior Organization," n.d. Available at http://www.collectionscanada.gc.ca.

of those entrusted with the authority to make decisions on behalf of the citizenry.

Tip: Always Respect Ministerial Authority

Public servants must separate their own personal agendas from the government's agenda. Public servants do not have the right to determine what is in the public's interest, or to judge what makes for good public policy. Ministers do.

The Division of Power

The nuances of Canadian government are not obvious even to those who have spent a lifetime working in public administration.[4]

Understanding how government works begins by recognizing that political power is derived from the Canadian constitution—a body of written documents, unwritten conventions, and key court rulings that organize government and society. Primary among these rules, the *Constitution Acts* outline how government authority is distributed within and among governments, while the *Charter of Rights and Freedoms* legally enshrines citizens' civil and political rights.

Canada is a parliamentary democracy with a constitutional monarchy. The King or Queen of Great Britain is the King or Queen of Canada.[5] The monarch and the Crown are represented in Ottawa by the *governor general*, and the governor general appoints a *lieutenant governor* to represent the Crown in each provincial capital. Commissioners fulfil a similar role in the territories. These individuals' responsibilities as the *Crown* largely encompass ceremonial functions, such as ribbon cutting. More substantively, they give assent to bills and have the power to appoint and dismiss governments. The governor general and lieutenants are on standby to act as safeguards in the unlikely event they need to uphold constitutional principles in the face of inappropriate government requests.

New hires in the public service are asked to take an oath signifying their duty to the government of the day and loyalty to the Crown. For instance, a new employee in the Government of Canada will be asked by a member of the Public Service Commission or delegate to make the following statement as a condition of employment:

> I swear (or solemnly affirm) that I will faithfully and honestly fulfil the duties that devolve on me by reason of my employment in the public service of Canada and that I will not, without due authority, disclose or make known any matter that comes to my knowledge by reason of such employment.[6]

As well, a confidentiality agreement may need to be signed. Some employees, such as co-operative education students, may be asked to repeat the oath (or affirmation) at the conclusion of their employment.

Canada has a *federal* system of government. Legislative power is divided between a national (federal) government and 10 provincial governments. Section 91 of the *Constitution Act, 1867* assigns authority to the Government of Canada for areas including the military, postal service, immigration, and many economic instruments such as currency, banking, and trade. Section 92 provides provincial governments with authority over lands, hospitals, municipalities, education, non-renewable resources, and many forms of licensing. The three territories are within the constitutional jurisdiction of the federal government. Their powers are delegated by Parliament.

Provincial governments are largely similar in structure to the federal government. A key difference is that the Parliament of Canada has two legislative chambers: the House of Commons and the Senate. Each provincial legislature has a single assembly, meaning bills pass through provincial systems much more quickly but with a lot less scrutiny than in Ottawa. This is because for the Queen's representative to sign a bill into law, it must be introduced to members of the legislature (first reading), be debated and referred to committee for study (second reading), and voted upon by members (third reading). A federal bill must pass through all three readings in both the House of Commons and the Senate. A provincial bill must pass through just one legislative chamber. As well, the provincial committee review system may be less rigorous than it is in Ottawa.

Canada's constitutional order includes Indigenous peoples' inherent right to self-government.[7] By virtue of centuries of settler colonialism, First Nations, Métis, and Inuit communities exercise this right to a varied, but overall limited, extent. For instance, while Aboriginal and treaty rights are protected in other parts of the constitution, jurisdiction over "Indians and lands reserved for Indians" remains entrenched in section 91. Many observers view these and other legal principles as subjugating Indigenous people to the authority of the federal government. This was borne out in the establishment of residential schools as a means of assimilating Indigenous people into Canadian society. The Truth and Reconciliation Commission's (TRC) 2015 report revealed the intergenerational impact of the personal abuse inflicted by the schools and what it called a cultural genocide.[8] Governments across Canada have committed to addressing the TRC's 94 calls to action. All public servants must come to terms with the issues raised by the Commission. Many are beginning to do so.

TRC call to action #57 recommends the establishment of mandatory Indigenous awareness training for public servants. These learning experiences are designed to ensure all public servants understand Indigenous people's historic and contemporary realities. It is hoped public servants will develop increased knowledge around the challenges and opportunities facing Indigenous people in Canada. A public service with a deeper cultural understanding will be able to address these issues more effectively and help foster mutual respect among Indigenous and non-Indigenous people.

Tip: Explore Indigenous Learning Opportunities
Developing Indigenous awareness, sensitivity, and competency is a lifelong process. Experiential learning opportunities like the KAIROS Blanket Exercise walk participants through Canadian-Indigenous history using hands-on activities and interaction with Elders. With narrators telling the story of colonization, participants take on the role of Indigenous people and begin to appreciate what it might feel like to have their land (blankets) and even children (dolls) taken away from them.

The Main Institutions of Government

Democratic elements are found throughout Canada's parliamentary system of government. Elections are held to elect representatives to the House of Commons and to provincial and territorial assemblies. The constitution allows up to five years between elections, but legislation requiring an election every four years is common, and voting is more frequent when less than half of the members of the legislature belong to the governing party. The leader of the political party that has the support of a majority of elected members is appointed by the Crown's representative to lead the government. In Ottawa, the provinces, and Yukon, the *first minister* (i.e., prime minister or premier) is the party leader who commands the confidence of the legislative assembly to govern. This individual forms a *cabinet*, usually by choosing some elected members of the governing party to serve as *ministers*. A minister's role typically involves providing political leadership for a department, agency, and/or office. Ministers who are members of the assembly are separately accountable for representing citizens in their respective electoral districts. This appointment process does not apply to Nunavut and the Northwest Territories, which do not have political parties. Their system of consensus government involves members of the legislature selecting the premier and cabinet ministers from their own ranks.

First ministers pick members of their cabinets for a host of different reasons. Ensuring that each region is represented around the cabinet table is often a primary imperative. So is socio-demographic balance in terms of gender, Indigeneity, language, ethnicity, age, and other factors. A member's political experience is valued. In some portfolios, such as justice and finance, a particular professional skill set may be sought. Then there are political considerations, including rewarding personal loyalty to the leader and raising the profile of members in swing ridings.

The cabinet is the executive branch of government—the source of most political decision-making. Cabinet decisions are often translated as minutes in council for the public service to carry out. To manage the volume and importance of business, each government usually maintains a number of cabinet committees. Small groups of ministers meet to study an issue and make recommendations to cabinet as a whole. Some cabinet committees are permanent, such as the Treasury Board, which oversees how government raises and spends its funds. Others are temporary and are created by the first minister to address a topical issue. All ministers must publicly support cabinet decisions. This principle of cabinet solidarity ensures a measure of collective responsibility and prevents ministers from disowning unpopular decisions.

> **Tip: Adjust Your Approaches When the Government Changes**
> The line between politically astute advice and partisan support is blurriest immediately before, during, and after an election period. If a new government is formed, public servants must assess how aligned their thinking may have become with the approach of the previous government.

A bit of a grey area is the existence of *parliamentary secretaries*, known as associate ministers in some jurisdictions. They do not normally have cabinet status. The role is best seen as a training ground for elected representatives who one day might be appointed to cabinet. A parliamentary secretary rarely attends cabinet meetings or participates in decision-making. Rather, they attend to matters delegated by the minister they are assigned to assist. They typically ease the workload on a busy portfolio or address a priority focus for government. For instance, a parliamentary secretary might deliver speeches or handle enquiries during question period. All of this is done on behalf of the minister, who might be busy with other matters or have political reasons for delegating a task.

The political executive is held to account by the members of a legislature. In Ottawa, the legislative branch is composed of Members of Parliament (MPs) and Senators. In the provinces, elected representatives are commonly known as Members of the Legislative Assembly (MLAs), with some variations: Ontario has Members of Provincial Parliament (MPPs), Quebec has Members of the National Assembly (MNAs), and in Newfoundland and Labrador there are Members of the House of Assembly (MHAs). Members of the legislature belonging to the same political party regularly convene in caucus meetings. Bringing everyone together is an opportunity to exchange information in private and to project unity in public.

Not all decisions flow through cabinet. A minister may make policy decisions in a department when the legal authority exists to do so. Executive decisions are normally channelled to the public service through the *deputy minister* (DM). The deputy is the most senior public servant in the department and its bureaucratic head. Assistant and associate deputy ministers (ADMs) oversee certain areas within a department, such as the policy group, corporate affairs, or operations. Each area employs directors to whom managers report, who themselves oversee analysts, and so on. The Government of Canada is so large that directors report to directors general who report to ADMs. It is the role of these public servants to provide information up the line and to act on directives. If mistakes are made, the minister is accountable to the prime minister (or premier) and the legislature through the concept of ministerial responsibility, discussed in **Chapter 4**. Most ministers seek media coverage for positive initiatives of their department. Conversely, the minister is the departmental spokesperson when there is a controversial decision or blunder. Public servants must be aware of organizational hierarchies (see Figure 2 for an example of a provincial hierarchy).

The executive branch of government is more extensive than cabinet and ministers. Information about the whole of government flows

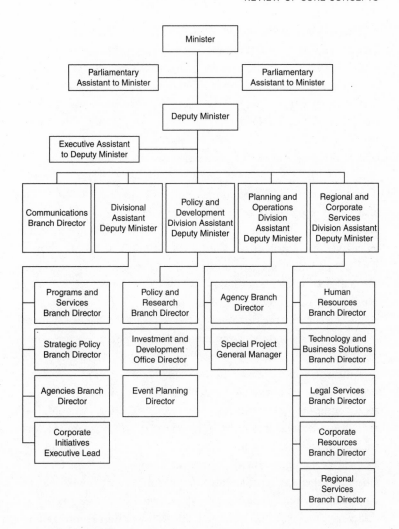

FIGURE 2 Hierarchy in a Large Provincial Government Department

Source: Adapted from Ontario Ministry of Tourism, Culture, and Sport, "Ministry Organization Chart," 2011. Available at http://www.mtc.gov.on.ca/en/about/rbp_2011_12._org_chart.shtml.

through two main central offices. So much power is concentrated in the Prime Minister's Office (PMO) or a Premier's Office that their political staff exercise considerable authority. The chief of staff is the most senior political staffer and is understood to speak for the prime minister or premier. Expectations are that ministers, their political staff, deputy ministers, and others will fall in line with requests made by the PMO or Premier's Office.

Those central agencies and ministers' offices, as well as the public service itself, are assisted by nonpartisan public servants in the Privy Council Office (PCO). At the provincial level this is sometimes called the Executive Council Office (ECO). The PCO/ECO provides nonpartisan support at the highest level of government. These public servants deliver briefings to the first minister, coordinate cabinet operations, conduct cross-sector policy analysis, prepare speeches, and so forth. Those offices are led by the most senior public servant, the *clerk*, who also serves as secretary to cabinet. The role of the clerk has three components: head of the public service, supporting the first minister as head of government, and supporting the functions of cabinet. The clerk oversees the government's deputy ministers. These public servants serve at the pleasure of the cabinet. Each deputy works with a minister and can exercise that minister's applicable authority. Deputy ministers report to the first minister via the clerk. Collectively, these senior personnel and their staff ensure that the public service delivers the agenda of the government; ensure policy coordination across government; and participate in the implementation of cabinet decisions, document control, and executive-level briefings.

Together the prime minister or premier, cabinet, the chief of staff, and the clerk sit atop each government's organizational pyramid. The political staff and senior public servants working in the PCO/ECO and other central agencies (including Finance and Treasury Board Secretariat) are commonly known as the *centre* of government.[9] Ministers, deputy ministers, and departmental staff are expected to follow requests from the centre. This is illustrated in Figure 3. The PMO or Premier's Office maintains close contact with political staff in each minister's office to ensure government directives are understood and implemented. The PCO/ECO has a similar relationship with deputy ministers' offices across government, with the clerk and staff coordinating work with DM colleagues. In this environment, deputy ministers are expected to work collaboratively with their respective ministers, and with the clerk and fellow deputies.[10] DMs are leaders within their own departments, coordinating various assistant deputy ministers who, in turn, must work with their directors general or executive directors. We return to this topic in **Chapter 4**.

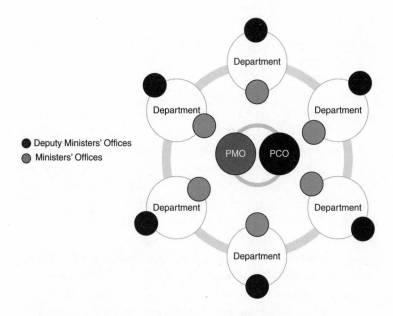

FIGURE 3 Visualizing the Power Structure in Westminster Governments

Executive accountability is where the parliamentary system becomes complex. According to Westminster traditions, on which Canada's system is based, cabinet is to be held to account by the legislature. In effect, two branches of government are fused because most if not all members of cabinet are simultaneously members of both the executive and the legislative branches. The level of public oversight may be suspect given the prevalence of majority governments and the strength of party discipline. On the other hand, the executive is held to account in closed-door caucus meetings and through votes in the legislature. In practice, the implications for the public service are that the first minister—and, by extension, political staff in the PMO or Premier's Office—exercise influence and control over cabinet, ministers, and departments.

Thus, the first minister and other ministers typically have seats in the very institution that is meant to hold them to account. Among the resulting conventions is an expectation of strict party discipline. Elected representatives are expected to publicly support the leader of their party. This can and does lead to a united public front against members of other parties. In reality, parliamentarians, including members of cabinet, are often on good terms with a number of their colleagues across the aisle.

The cabinet must have the support of the legislative branch. This principle of responsible government helps to ensure that a majority of the people's elected representatives approve of what the cabinet is doing. The legislative branch scrutinizes and votes on how government raises and spends money. It is a forum to discuss issues of the day and to debate and approve bills introduced by ministers and private members. Parliamentarians can register their disapproval by voting down major policy, such as the annual budget. Alternatively, a motion of non-confidence in the government can be introduced. When a non-confidence motion passes, the governor general or lieutenant governor typically dissolves the legislature. A general election is held to elect representatives to the legislature, some of whom will be appointed to form a new cabinet.

A majority government exists when more than half the members of the legislature are affiliated with one party. It allows the governing party to implement an agenda with little concern for opposition parties' opinions. Conversely, in a minority government situation, the risk of a snap election creates instability. This makes governing more difficult because the governing party needs to pay more attention to opposition opinion. In practice, running a government without assured control of the legislative assembly is more problematic than it might seem.[11] There is a constant threat of an election and excessive short-term thinking. Both scenarios have implications for how the government operates and for the work of public servants.

Even during a minority government situation, members of other political parties have limited power. The party with the second highest number of seats is termed the Official Opposition. The leader of the opposition designates a shadow cabinet, whereby some opposition members of the legislature formally act as public critics for given ministers. In the legislature, the main tools that opposition parties wield are holding the government to account through question period and legislative committees. They may use procedural delay to frustrate the ability of the government party to pass bills in a timely manner. Outside the legislature, the leader of the Official Opposition commands media attention, as do the leaders of any other parties. Their perspectives often disrupt government plans but on the whole help to ensure that a variety of viewpoints are considered in public policy decisions.

Many members of the legislature who are affiliated with the governing party do not have a formal role in the executive. They are known as backbenchers because, as a sign of their lesser role, their chairs literally fill out the back spots in a legislative chamber. Members of cabinet and opposition critics occupy the front benches. Most backbenchers prioritize providing service to their constituents and promote the government's achievements.

Canada's constitution stipulates that provincial legislatures have exclusive authority to make laws about municipalities. Forms of local government vary considerably. They range from cities, towns, and villages, to counties, townships, and special-purpose bodies. Each has its own unique governance structure, internal dynamics, and way of dealing with other levels of government. Power tends to be concentrated at the top of the organization—within the office of the mayor, an executive committee, or city council.

Local politics and elections are likewise different from place to place. The virtual absence of political parties is the most significant difference, except in places such as Montreal and Vancouver. Decision-making processes depend largely on the size of the community and whether representatives are elected to represent geographic constituencies (e.g., wards) or on an at-large basis (e.g., an entire city or town). Some local governments have committee systems to support the decision-making process. As a result, the role of public servants in local government resembles that of their federal/provincial/territorial colleagues in some ways, and differs in others.[12]

Be careful not to assume that all municipalities are governed the same way. For example, Montreal's population is over 1.7 million, and Montrealers elect a mayor and 64 councillors to oversee an annual operating budget of approximately $5 billion. Just four people live in Tilt Cove, Newfoundland: one is mayor, two are councillors, and one is town clerk.[13] The population of Tilt Cove nearly triples in the summer when people occupy cottages there. In Montreal, the clerk is a highly paid senior public servant who oversees the city's bureaucracy. In Tilt Cove, the clerk is paid for one hour a week, including for curbside garbage collection.

Whether at the local or national level, the decisions and actions of all legislative bodies and governments are subject to legal interpretation. In Canada, the rule of law is essential for an orderly, well-functioning civil society. Nobody is above the law, including those holding high office. To preserve this principle, the constitution and laws are interpreted by the judicial branch. All laws passed by a legislature must be compliant with the constitution, including the *Charter of Rights and Freedoms*. Activists and other citizens sometimes initiate court challenges to test the constitutionality of legislation. Judges may find that a law does not adequately address a situation. They might make legal interpretations that differ with public opinion, create law where one does not exist, or refer an issue to the legislature to ensure a law is constitutional.[14] In this way, the rule of law rises above partisan politics, as the judicial branch weighs legal arguments away from political theatre.

The Supreme Court of Canada is the final court of appeal and sets out the ultimate interpretation of the constitution. Supreme Court justices are appointed by the governor general on the advice of the prime minister. Similar processes occur at the provincial level for lower court judges. Idealistically, this results in nonpartisan appointments when an independent appointments commission or similar process is in place. In reality, appointees to the bench hold similar values as the governing party. Historically the Supreme Court has made many monumental decisions on a host of topics. This includes hot-button issues punted by politicians to the judiciary through reference cases, such as same-sex marriage.

With this general overview of how Canada is governed, our attention now turns to how public servants operate within these broad parameters.

Chapter Takeaways

This chapter establishes that public servants play an important, but highly structured, role in Canadian democracy.

- Public servants serve Canadian citizens and society. They are directly accountable to their superiors, and ultimately to their ministers and the Crown.

- Public servants do not make public policy decisions. They provide advice to elected officials and implement the directives they receive from cabinet.
- Public servants are part of a complex system of government. To perform effectively and avoid overstepping their authority, they must understand how their responsibilities intersect with elected, appointed, and partisan officials from all three branches of government (executive, legislative, judicial).

Notes

1   This number encompasses federal, provincial, and municipal governments, and all of their agencies, boards, and commissions. This includes health, social service, and post-secondary institutions. It does not include primary and secondary school teachers, nurses, law enforcement, or other public sector workers. See Statistics Canada (2012).

2   Canada was ranked atop the 2017 International Civil Service Effectiveness (InCiSE) Index, which compared 31 national bureaucracies on measures ranging from fiscal and financial management to policymaking to inclusiveness and integrity. See InCiSE (2017).

3   For example, see Mueller (1999).

4   For an overview of government operations in Canada, see Forsey (2005).

5   For simplicity, we do not delve into the formalities of the Crown. For more information, see Smith (2013).

6   Public Service Employment Act, http://lois-laws.justice.gc.ca/eng/acts/P-33.01/FullText.html.

7   For more detail, see Coulthard (2014).

8   MacDonald (2015).

9   Savoie (1999).

10   For more information about the role of deputy ministers, see Canada (2017).

11   Russell (2008).

12   For further discussion, see Sancton (2011).

13   Butterfield (2017).

14   See, for example, Hiebert (2002).

CHAPTER 2

THE PUBLIC SECTOR BARGAIN

Yes, Minister is a classic British sitcom about the tensions between politicians and public servants. Lessons from the show remain poignant for Canadian public servants today. The minister is portrayed as idealistic and naïve; the deputy minister as pragmatic and manipulative. A third character, Bernard, is an impartial public servant who embodies the more noble features of the bureaucracy. In one scene, the minister complains about all the correspondence needing attention. Bernard proposes a solution: he will thank each sender on behalf of the minister and will say that the matter is either under consideration or is under active consideration. The minister, perplexed, asks what the difference is. "Well, under consideration means we've lost the file. Under active consideration means we're trying to find it," Bernard explains.[1]

The timeless nature of scenes like these resonate most with those who relate to the mundane nature of most bureaucratic work and the power struggles in high levels of officialdom. Like the writers of *Yes, Minister,* or more recently *W1A, Veep,* or *The Beaverton,* they recognize that how public administration and politics operate is very different than theorists' ideals.

It takes a bit of effort to see the practical application of scholarly theories and how they can offer useful, on-the-ground guidance. "That works well in practice, but does it work in theory?" is a running punchline among public servants working on complex, time-sensitive files. Nonetheless, theory is crucial to the study and practice of public administration. In particular, as we indicated in **Chapter 1**, seminal theorists depict a so-called "bargain" between a professional public service and ministers. The former is expected to offer policy advice and then implement directives from the latter. In return for their impartial service, public servants receive competitive compensation and job security. This agreement has evolved over time, but the concept drives our understanding of how government should and does work.

Government as an Organization

To understand how government operates, let alone your own role within it, you need some awareness of the theoretical principles upon which public administration is based. Within the public service, it is said that theory is when you know everything but nothing works; practice is when everything works, but no one knows why; and when theory and practice are combined, nothing works, and no one knows why. Put another way, theory without real-life testing has limited value, and practice without theoretical understanding is haphazard.

> **Tip: Be Inquisitive and Request Guidance**
> If you are unsure of something at work, ask questions and seek clarification. Chances are you'll be glad you did.

Theories become popular for a reason. Enduring ones have been applied repeatedly to phenomena over time and around the world. Theories draw out the commonalities and explain patterns and trends. They help us simplify, explain, categorize, and even predict events. They anchor new ideas and assist in the interpretation of statistics. Theoretical models, diagrams, concepts, and terminology are the currency of public administration. When something happens, drawing on theoretical knowledge helps an astute observer to arrive at informed judgments. Thus, being familiar with theories of public administration can help us understand the nature of government and public service.

What follows is a summary of some important theories and frameworks. This overview of seminal ideas will help you understand, communicate, and address some of the organizational challenges that public servants have faced for centuries.

A longstanding way of thinking about how government is organized was developed by German sociologist Max Weber in the 1800s.[2] He maintained that it is imperative that governments operate in a highly efficient manner. The characteristics of a *Weberian bureaucracy* are recognizable in Canada today. There must be an organizational hierarchy with employees following a chain of command. There must be formal rules, and employees must operate within those boundaries. Public servants must be specialists who can apply their expertise to a variety of situations. The government must be impersonal to ensure that staff in similar situations are treated in a reasonably identical manner, without favouritism. Thus, there must be standardized hiring and firing, which brings job security for those fulfilling their roles. Ideally this should produce a functional workplace that values specialized skill sets. The traits of a Weberian bureaucracy result in a distinct organizational culture that operates in an environment of norms and processes. It can produce an impersonal workplace.

Conversely, *political staff* often arrive in government from the campaign trail and/or the private sector where bureaucratic norms are constantly challenged if not ignored.[3] They have hardbound loyalties to one another. They have been on the front lines of interacting with Canadians and calls for change. Their expectations and demands of the public service can be idealistic and uninformed, perhaps even contrary to professional codes of values for public servants.[4] Navigating the two different worlds is among the foremost challenges of political personnel seeking to advance an agenda—and likewise for public servants who want a successful career.

This is where politics and public administration collide, with mixed results. The public service has its own organizational culture. Even though they are all on the public payroll, public servants hired through the merit principle work in a different organizational environment than do ministers and political staff, who are political appointments. Public servants are anonymous, nonpartisan, cautious, and follow lengthy consultation processes; political personnel are public figures to varying degrees, are hyper-partisan, are risk takers and prioritize immediacy. One group is relatively permanent, allowing them to engage in longer-term planning and implementation, and the other impermanent and impatient. These characteristics inform some of the core dynamics within a bureaucracy.

Among the more basic understandings of how public administration works relates to the permanency of the civil service. In 1887, Woodrow Wilson, who would go on to become president of the United States, published a seminal article about government.[5] He believed that public servants must be accountable to the politicians who are in turn held to account by the electorate. Wilson wrestled with the role of politics in government and concluded that politics is what sets the agenda. It falls to public servants to implement that agenda irrespective of their personal political views.

A century later, Wilson's separation of administration from politics broadened into what became known as the Schafferian bargain. In the 1970s, British scholar Bernard Schaffer reflected on parliamentary government.[6] He concluded that public servants must do the bidding of their political masters while upholding their legal obligations and public administration standards. In return, ministers are the public face of the government, and are held accountable to the electorate that they serve. Ministers communicate and promote what they believe to be politically important. They publicly explain policies, receive credit for good news, and bear the brunt of blame when there are problems.

A public service bargain allows government employees to work away from the media spotlight with a common understanding of the ground rules. Public servants benefit from job security compared with the relative precariousness of political jobs and employment in other sectors. They enjoy competitive compensation, including salary and pensions. Their employer engages in merit-based hiring and promotion practices in return for loyal, politically neutral service to the government of the day. Public servants should therefore avoid blatant political interference in personnel decisions or distribution of government resources.

Schaffer's opinion that public servants should toil in obscurity supports the underlying principles advanced by Weber. However, constitutional protections of democratic rights combined with the ability to communicate via social media are putting some pressure on traditional views of a quiet, anonymous public service. Should public servants be allowed to say what they like on social media in their private time? Or, as a condition of employment, should they be expected to represent the government at all times? Should their private advice be subject to freedom of information requests? Where you stand might depend on where you sit.

Threats to the Public Service Bargain

Concern about the sanctity of the public service bargain has been voiced since Schaffer first proposed the idea.[7] Most of the scholarly anxiety is about how corporate thinking and political personnel invade the sanctum of public administration. There is debate about the extent to which bureaucrats are answerable to ministers and the public through legislative committees (see **Chapter 4**). In the parliamentary system there are added concerns that so much attention is paid to party leaders, especially to the first minister. All of this has political and practical consequences.

The corporate-style delivery of public services represents what British scholar Christopher Hood dubs *New Public Management* (NPM).[8] The NPM trend was spurred by a quest for efficiencies and a private sector approach to organizing government. It encompasses the shrinking of government, privatization, automation of public services, businesslike management, performance measurement, and emphasis on results. The benefits of NPM include its politically neutral nature and the freedom of managers to resolve situations, often known by the mantra of "let the managers manage." Criticisms include suspicion about treating government like a business and doubt that a corporate mentality can be implemented in government.

The New Public Management philosophy led to a Canadian twist, one that is more sinister. In the early 2000s, Dalhousie University professor Peter Aucoin observed the politicization of public administration in Westminster systems, and grouped his observations as a *New Political Governance* (NPG) model.[9] The NPG model reflects the implications of an evolving media environment, public expectations of transparency, performance auditing, intensifying political competition, and a polarized electorate. Aucoin held that the public service is being politicized as a result of these environmental pressures and the resulting strategic manoeuvres by partisans. NPG submits that governance is fusing with campaigning; that political staff are displacing senior public servants as trusted advisors; that public servants are expected to personally support the government's agenda; and that as a consequence there is a general displacement of impartiality by partisanship. This brings to light the disagreement about whether public servants are as neutral, impartial, and dedicated to the public interest as theorists would hope. Invariably, political personnel believe that the bureaucracy has its own agenda, while public servants see themselves as trained professionals.

Ministers generally surround themselves with political staff who are astute. Politicos' desire to change the world often brings freshness and originality. They can be a healthy counterbalance to the slow, measured pace of government. Be careful, though: some political staff are unaware of the boundaries between politics, policy, and the public service bargain.

Those who study Canadian government exhibit less concern than their British counterparts do about the hiring of political advisors and consultants. Nevertheless, as Aucoin hinted, Canadian political parties leverage all available public resources to promote a political agenda and support their re-election. This is known as *permanent campaigning*. It reflects a philosophy that the next election is just around the corner and shows a competitive drive to win every public battle.[10] Political marketers encourage the government to focus on subsets of the electorate to whom they promote targeted messages. The use of relationship management data and the precision of social media communication is fostering this. These phenomena provide additional support for Aucoin's arguments about New Political Governance.

The research of Donald Savoie of the Université de Moncton reveals additional threats to the Schafferian ideal.[11] Savoie illustrates that the role of senior public servants has drifted from being politically neutral, expert, and anonymous advisors to ministers. As government becomes more transparent—through freedom-of-information requests and public appearances by deputy ministers at legislative committee hearings, for instance—bureaucrats' ability to deliver frank, even controversial, advice is compromised. At the same time, policymaking is an increasingly inter-sectoral affair. This limits the capacity and need for deputy ministers to be intimately connected with the work of their respective departments. Deputies are chief executives, reflecting the businesslike spirit of New Public Management. They are more adept at manoeuvring among their counterparts and key external stakeholders than at delivering in-depth advice on specific areas of policy.

> **Tip: Be Aware of Your Deputy Minister's Priorities**
>
> It's often said, "What interests my boss fascinates me." Most deputy ministers sign performance agreements with their clerk, outlining key policy, service, and corporate objectives for the year ahead. These objectives typically cascade down to subordinates' performance agreements. Knowing what your deputy is accountable for doing can help you shape your own priorities. Some executives openly share their performance agreements with staff who directly report to them. It's worth asking so you can align your own objectives and priorities.

Guiding Principles for Public Servants

So, if the public service bargain is under threat, what is a public servant to do? A general recommendation, and objective of this chapter, is to pique interest in public administration theory and encourage further reading. The maxim that knowledge is power applies. More broadly, public servants are well-advised to follow two prominent guideposts set out by thinkers such as Weber, Wilson, Schaffer, Aucoin, and Savoie:

1. offer fearless advice to your superiors, and
2. loyally implement your superiors' lawful directives.

The origins of the Canadian public servant's mantra to offer fearless advice and loyal implementation are unclear. Alex Himelfarb, former federal clerk, used the expression in a 2002 speech. He urged public servants to focus on core values of "integrity and excellence in everything we do; respect for people, citizens, employees, colleagues, elected officials; embracing diversity as a source of strength; linguistic duality; and adaptability."[12] Himelfarb highlighted the skill sets of public servants as "rigorous policy analysis, creative policy options, innovative service delivery, effective resource management always focussed on value for money, fearless advice, loyal implementation." Whatever the source, the expression captures a way of thinking that pervades many areas of public administration. It requires a bit of context.

The idea of offering fearless advice is sometimes erroneously confused with speaking truth to power. This is inaccurate because it implies public servants are the purveyors of truth. In reality, they offer information and recommendations. Advice is tainted by their own biases based on their training and as members of society. But the overall premise upholds the Weberian tradition. A public servant develops expertise and has job security for the purposes of conveying the best available information to those in higher positions. Informed opinions should be shared with honesty and without pandering to what others might want to hear. Ministers and high-ranking public servants do not generally have sufficient time, knowledge, skills, and/or authority to independently identify problems worth solving or solutions worth pursuing. They rely on rank-and-file analysts and managers to be creative and bold when it comes to identifying potential courses of action. Public servants must be detailed and forthcoming in terms of the potential risks and rewards involved. The vitality and responsiveness of modern government depends upon it.

Tip: Strive for Accuracy and Clarity
The New Zealand government offers wise advice to its policy analysts. Great briefings "identify all of the decisions needed ... are accurate in every detail; don't leave any room for doubt about what is being decided; make sense independently of the [background material]; [and] set out clear options for ministers to decide between."[13]

One standard way for public servants to convey advice is to collaborate on written materials intended for the minister and ministerial staff. There are many templates and instruments in government for compiling information in a succinct, consistent manner. A common tool is the *briefing note*, which is exactly what it seems: a tightly written summary that succinctly informs the reader about key subject material. It might request a decision or prepare for an event or situation. Briefing notes and their variants (e.g., information notes, synopses, and so on) are a means of conveying potentially complex information in a digestible manner.[14] They are prepared for busy executives who do not have time to read up about an issue but need to quickly become familiar with the major points and concepts. The author seeks to present as much useful information within the available space constraints as possible. This must be done in a reader-friendly manner that informs as well as enlightens. For instance, briefing notes often begin with a summary box of two to four bullet points. To maximize efficiency and the approvals process, there is typically a standardized presentation format. Summarizing an issue in a page or two is challenging for most public servants; yet, from the perspective of ministers, most briefing notes are neither brief nor noteworthy. They value briefings that are clear, precise, forceful, analytical, and based on both expertise and experience. See Table 1.

TABLE 1 Government of Canada Briefing Note "Do's and Don'ts"

BRIEFING NOTE DO'S	BRIEFING NOTE DON'TS
Audience	
• Know your reader's perspective and concerns. • Anticipate and answer your reader's questions.	• Don't assume that your reader has the same technical knowledge as you do.
Style	
• Keep it short: 2 pages maximum. • Be clear and concise: write sentences averaging 15-20 words up to a maximum of 30 words; write paragraphs of no more than 5-6 sentences, or 7-9 lines. • Use the active voice and action verbs.	• Don't use too many acronyms or abbreviations. • Stay away from jargon and technical terms (define them if you have to use them). • Avoid strings of nouns. • Avoid using too many adverbs and adjectives.

(continued)

TABLE 1 (*continued*)

BRIEFING NOTE DO'S	BRIEFING NOTE DON'TS
Organization and Structure	
• Get to the point quickly: present the most important information first (giving general information before specific).	• Don't include more than one idea for each paragraph.
• Put the right information in the right section.	• Don't introduce new elements or repeat information in the conclusion and recommendations.
• Present your rationale clearly and logically.	
• Present information in small and manageable chunks: use bullets and tables when needed.	
• Use appendices for details, but don't overdo it.	
Content	
• Be clear on the issue of the briefing note.	• Don't use ambiguous statements or vague timelines.
• Summarize what you want the reader to grasp quickly.	• Don't hide or diminish the seriousness of a problem or situation.
• Provide pertinent and complete information based on objective analysis and consultations.	• Avoid presenting unsubstantiated arguments.
• Make clear recommendations linked to facts.	• Refrain from giving your personal opinions: stick to concrete facts.
• State possible consequences when applicable.	• Don't overwhelm your reader with details.
Process	
• Make a plan and focus on the core issue: aim for quality arguments, not quantity of information.	• Don't write before you are clear on the objective of the request.
• Check all the facts.	• Don't start writing the summary before you finish writing the content of the briefing note.
• Be discerning when copying and pasting.	• Limit the number of changes made for reasons of style and personal preference.
• Discuss the proposed changes with the editors.	
• Learn from previous briefing notes.	

Source: Translation Bureau, Public Works and Government Services Canada, "Write Clear and Effective Briefing Notes," 2015. Available at http://www.btb.termiumplus.gc.ca/tpv2guides/guides/wrtps/index-eng.html?lang=eng&lettr=indx_catlog_c&page=9gi2AZ79TR4Y.html.

The fearless advice and loyal implementation mantra is noble and principled. Not everyone follows it. Some senior public servants benefit from telling ministers what they want to hear. The possibility that emails, briefing materials, and handwritten notes will be released through a freedom of information request means that some public servants are hesitant to provide frank advice.[15] They elect for verbal briefings over written communication. This compromises the collaborative nature of preparing briefs and brings into question the precision of information and institutional memory. Loyal implementation is nuanced as well. Public servants must be politically neutral, report to government not the opposition, follow a chain of command, and obey orders given by those with the legal authority to do so. Ethics of the public service are discussed in **Chapter 5**.

Chapter Takeaways

This chapter argues that theories of governance and public administration are important tools for public servants to preserve their proper place in the complex, dynamic world of public administration.

- Theorist Max Weber helps us appreciate the merits of hierarchy in the public service. Woodrow Wilson advocated the importance of separating the roles of partisan and nonpartisan officials in service of the government's agenda.
- These concepts coalesce into the public service bargain. It holds that public servants receive relatively generous terms of employment in return for providing high-quality, loyal service to the government of the day.
- Various elements of the public service bargain fall under threat from time to time. This is acute when lines of accountability are blurred, modes of public sector management diverge from the core principles of parliamentary democracy, or when certain benefits of employment are called into question.
- Public servants must be versed in the theoretical foundations of public administration to ensure they play an appropriate and effective role in Canadian democracy.

Notes

1 Hogan (2016). See also Brodie (2012).

2 See, for example, Udy (1959).

3 Wilson (2016).

4 Such as the federal Values and Ethics Code for the Public Sector. See https://www.tbs-sct.gc.ca/pol/doc-eng.aspx?id=25049.

5 Wilson (1887).

6 Schaffer (1973).

7 Hood and Dixon (2015), 29.

8 Aucoin (1995).

9 Aucoin (2012).

10 For example, see Marland, Giasson, and Esselment (2017).

11 Savoie (2003).

12 Himelfarb (2002).

13 Cabinet Office (2010).

14 For more, see Savard and Melançon (2014).

15 Gingras (2012).

CHAPTER 3

THE POLITICS OF PUBLIC POLICY

Turn on the TV, visit a news website, or check your newsfeed. Chances are you will see a dramatic call for government to take action. Protesters marching with signs and banners. Commentators offering scathing critiques of the prime minister or premier. The leaders of political parties, businesses, unions, interest groups—all of them arguing about what government should or should not do. The public sphere is filled with organizations and people clamouring for public resources and changes to laws. They want their demands met—immediately. Day after day, week after week. How do politicians and public servants process all of this?

Some attempts to sway government are successful, while others fall flat. Prime Minister Justin Trudeau has said that government decisions are not made by "those who shout the loudest."[1] Elected officials must decide which of these calls deserve government attention. But who decides *how* to address them? Developing the finer details of public policy is seen as the purview of professional public servants—as distinct from their elected, politically motivated masters.

Policy is the complex set of choices that a government makes on behalf of their citizens. This encompasses domestic policies (economic, environmental, social) and foreign policies (aid, defence, diplomacy, trade). Public servants have considerable expertise in these fields. But the policy direction that is obvious and appropriate to them is rarely how things turn out. A public servant's advice is just one element within many layers of formal and informal inputs that inform public policy. In this sense, policy is deeply political, and involves a web of interactions. In this chapter, we delve into the politics and processes of it all.

What Is Public Policy?

If politics is the practice of power, policy is its translation into action. The most famous definition of public policy is that it is "whatever governments choose to do or not to do."[2] Another variation is that public policy constitutes "what government ought or ought not do, and does or does not do"[3] when shaping the economy and society in pursuit of the public good. Governments' policy motivations come from many sources. Some are motivated by partisanship or ideology, others by regionalism, pragmatism, expediency, or some combination of these and other factors.

Most policy decisions involve assessing how to distribute finite resources, such as wealth, or how to regulate citizen behaviour. Public policies strive to improve community, though of course there is discord about what constitutes an improvement, let alone how to achieve it. Policies reflect the needs of diverse populations, such as the policy of official bilingualism in the Governments of Canada and New Brunswick, and unilingual service in all other jurisdictions, including French in Quebec.

Policymakers have several tools at their disposal. They can tax certain behaviours or establish regulations to curb them, potentially prioritizing the revenue that is generated. Consider government approaches to alcohol, cannabis, and tobacco consumption. Alternatively, they can establish incentive programs or create subsidies to encourage citizens to change how they behave. Here, retirement and children's educational savings programs come to mind. Nudging might occur through a non-forced approach, by promoting transparency or educating the public, as with product labelling. Policymakers could choose to combine these approaches, creating a system of incentives and disincentives. Policy choices also include strategy. For instance, sweeping change might be unpalatable, so instead a series of incremental changes are introduced. Alternatively, choosing to do nothing about a problematic policy signals that the status quo is supported.

Democratic societies like Canada foster a diversity of viewpoints. People debate how best to define the public good, how to determine what to prioritize, and how to achieve it. Public policy choices reward certain types of citizens with resources that enable them to meet their objectives. Policymaking is about trade-offs—choosing a position while recognizing the benefits and downsides of that choice.

In designing the process through which those rules are determined, ministers and public servants wield considerable power.

Expectations for objective and informed policymaking are persistent. Expanding knowledge, improved skills and computing capacity, evolving norms of transparency, new communications technology, and a changing citizenry have implications for policy development. So do the size of government, the number of policies, the competing political pressures, and the complexity of issues. Globalization adds additional considerations, such as the rules contained within international agreements. Navigating these complexities is challenging and time-consuming. Yet, cabinet and political staff want their policy priorities to move forward without undue delay. This political urgency creates real pressure on public servants to deliver quality advice under tight timelines.

Smooth decision-making requires a well-organized process. This extends beyond the Weberian bureaucracy discussed in **Chapter 2**. Governments develop procedures that result in routine decision-making.[4] Some policies are reasonably straightforward and repetitive, such as administering the renewal of a licence, or establishing whether someone qualifies for a benefit. In those instances, once a policy direction is set, public servants find the most effective ways of implementing or delivering it. Other times processes are more complicated. An existing policy may suddenly require revisiting, due to extraordinary individual circumstances or evolving public preferences, or perhaps a court ruling. Sometimes ministers and their staff bypass normal procedures in the name of political expediency, with or without input from public servants. This shortcutting may be benign or opportunistic. All of this complexity makes it difficult to neatly compartmentalize how public policy is developed and refined.

The Public Policy Cycle

Generally speaking, public policy travels along a cycle.[5] Proposed solutions to a public problem move along various common stages. These are presented in Figure 4.

Arguably the most political of these phases is the starting point, known as *agenda setting*. Each day, problems and solutions are promoted

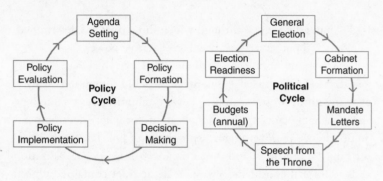

FIGURE 4 The Policy Cycle and the Political Cycle

by any number of political actors in any number of venues. The governing party sets the agenda with its election platform. Those promises are formalized as ministerial mandate letters, throne speeches, and the budget. Among many other tactics, opposition parties push alternatives; editors and producers exercise control over news media; citizens and interest groups organize protests and social media campaigns; academics and think tanks release reports; and lobbyists persuade key decision-makers behind closed doors. Within government, public servants scan the political environment and deliver briefings. The competition for attention highlights priority areas of concern. Media attention prompts a search by decision-makers for the best way to solve the alleged public problem. Consequently, at any given time some issues are positioned near the top of a government's list of priorities, while the rest are lower down the list. Public policy issues on the agenda get attention and resources; the others must wait, perhaps indefinitely. This is what makes agenda-setting so important. Even so, some government activities persist regardless of political noise: hospital patients will continue to receive three meals a day irrespective of cabinet priorities, for instance.

Just how are these centralized agendas set? It often starts with the governing party's most recent election platform. That political document outlines the party's commitments to the electorate should they be chosen to form a government. Some of the proposals were developed by the party membership in a policy convention and were subsequently tweaked by the leader's campaign strategists. Other proposals were designed largely by those strategists. If public servants are fortunate, the government's platform was crafted by experienced

policy experts with governance in mind and an expectation of implementation. Such platforms are often pre-assessed by policy experts to
itemize how much the commitments will cost and how long they will
take to implement. Governing parties seeking re-election who campaign
on their most recent speech from the throne or budget have benefit-
ted from the public service input. Even with those qualities, it can
take weeks or months for top-level bureaucrats and cabinet ministers
to identify key priorities and timelines following an election.

Tip: Explore the Poltext Archives
Platforms are prone to vanish after election night. Try visiting
Poltext (www.poltext.org), maintained by Université Laval.
Poltext archives platforms, throne and budget speeches, auditor
general reports, ministerial mandate letters, and more.

Major policy priorities appear in mandate letters from the prime
minister (or premier) to ministers. The letters are often posted online.
Most of the content is drawn from the campaign platform, but some
commitments change or emerge based on post-election discussions
with the public service. Priorities and timelines are further formalized
in the government's first speech from the throne and budget speech,
and in related strategic plans. In Ottawa, the throne speech is prepared
by the PMO and the PCO, approved by the prime minister, and delivered by the governor general. In the provinces, lieutenant governors,
premiers' offices, and Executive Council Offices fulfil similar roles.
Budget speeches fall under the purview of ministers of finance, advised
by the department of finance and other central agencies, subject to the
approval of the first minister. Most public servants have limited influence over such documents, particularly given their confidential nature.

These political documents inform the drafting of ministry business
plans, also known as departmental plans. Those strategies drill down
further in terms of the specific priorities and actions to be pursued over
the next year to five years. Once the Treasury Board approves a business plan, each applicable minister is accountable to the legislature for
delivering on the commitments. This accountability occurs through
the annual budget estimates process when ministers appear with their
executive personnel at applicable legislative committees to defend their

goals and records. Public servants further down the chain of command often develop operations plans to support these business plans. This adds further structure to the process of implementing the government's agenda.

> **Tip: Monitor Major Government Speeches**
> Pay careful attention to throne and budget speeches. They are more than spectacle. They contain carefully worded statements of the government's direction.

Illustrated in Figure 5, the development and implementation of a government's agenda proceeds through several phases. Public servants should be aware of each step in the process, from formulation to articulation to execution, archiving key documents as they are released.

Deputy ministers communicate shifts in a government's agenda and priorities to public servants. This information is publicized through public statements and annual budgets, necessitating adjustments to business plans. Changes to departmental planning are sparked by a host of factors, many of which are outside the government's direct control. Natural disasters force governments to reallocate funding and personnel to response and recovery efforts. Likewise, resource reallocation is required in the event of sudden shifts in government revenues brought about by international market forces. Opposition parties, other governments, advocacy groups, the media, and various political actors may place pressure on the government to change course. The resignation of a first minister and change of government prompts an overhaul of priorities—even the words and phrases used by public servants must evolve. All told, public servants

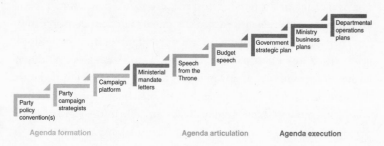

FIGURE 5 Operationalizing the Government's Agenda

must be attuned to the broader political environment in order to anticipate possible changes in the government's agenda.

> **Tip: Align Your Priorities with Cabinet Priorities**
> Speak the language of the government of the day. For instance, if the government is focused on outcomes and value for money, then internal and public documents should communicate this emphasis.

If a prime minister, premier, minister, deputy minister, or other powerful actor decides that an issue warrants such examination, the next phase is policy formulation. This entails the identification and ranking of policy actions. Policy formulation involves gathering information, consulting with others, and analyzing choices. The policy solutions found in academic journals or trending on social media may be excellent. But these changes may be idealistic or completely unworkable. Where will the money come from? What is our experience with this before? What are other jurisdictions doing? Who would benefit and who would suffer? Will there be different impacts on marginalized groups or regions? How is the issue playing out in the news? What do public opinion surveys say? Would the governing party's caucus support or oppose this? What about members of other political parties? These are just some of the countless political variables that factor into the policy formulation process. Some considerations are recurring and are so important that they are formalized in cabinet document templates. These policy lenses are discussed later in this chapter.

Decision-making occurs once a policy is formulated. At the departmental level, a minister has the executive authority to choose what action to take, though on some matters the deputy minister may act on behalf of the minister. Some decisions require cabinet approval, such as matters that cross into multiple portfolios. The ways that political decisions occur are outlined throughout this book. This includes whether to take any action whatsoever—recall that decisions for government to do nothing constitute public policy as well. These decisions are communicated in various ways. Common examples include the content of a speech from the throne, press conferences, social media posts, and news releases. On occasion, unconventional ways of announcing a decision occur, such as a minister using Twitter to inform a journalist of a policy.[6]

During the policy implementation phase, government resources are deployed to act on the policy decision. Implementation is difficult. One reason is the principal-agent problem. This concept holds that policy is not developed or implemented the way that decision-makers intend because it passes through so many hands.[7] The principal is the person(s) in charge who issues directives to agents (e.g., political staff and public servants) who are tasked with carrying out orders. At each iteration, agents shift the intended course of action somewhat. So a political party that promised in the election that they would do "X" finds that by the time the policy is announced by a minister it has become "Y" and that when it is actually delivered it becomes "Z." Some of this reflects the layers of expertise that public servants apply to a policy idea. But some of it is a source of considerable tension within government as ministers, political staff, management, and others negotiate the finer points of a policy initiative. A related problem is that public servants might not have the knowledge, skills, or resources to manage and deliver a government program or policy.

Finally, outcomes are monitored during policy evaluation. If complications are detected, information is fed back into the process to seek a decision on reforming a policy. Discontinuing a policy is less common because of the difficulty in defining failure and because the status quo may be beneficial for some members of society.[8] The extent of policy evaluation depends on the expertise and availability of resources. The nature of the decision-making structure within the government is another factor. Politics runs through this, too, because some cabinets are more interested in policy evaluation metrics than others.

As mentioned, public policy does not operate in a compact manner. It rarely travels the cycle in an orderly fashion from one stage to the next. The cycle may start at any point. Policymaking often skips stages or moves backward in response to external forces or government direction. Thought must be given to stages later in the cycle. Ideally, the personnel involved with implementing or evaluating a policy will be consulted when that policy is being formulated. But keep in mind that the policy cycle is an idealized process. Policymakers should aspire to follow it even if, as with many theories, this does not always reflect reality.

Indeed, the notion of an orderly policy cycle is grounded in a faulty assumption that policymakers are rational and have control over the process. Policymakers are part of a system in which objectives are seldom well-defined. The limits of time, funding, and expertise constrain the development of a comprehensive set of options and solid recommendations. For politicians and public servants alike, personal values shape the universe of facts presented. You may feel attached to a particular policy and do not agree with proposed changes. You may view the policy as part of a broader turf war with another unit or department. Moreover, actual evidence is limited, or selectively used. Furthermore, direction comes from varied sources of authority. In this sort of environment public servants should treat the policy cycle as a general guide to steer the process back on course. At a minimum they can recognize and mitigate the potential pitfalls they will likely encounter.

Other times, urgent situations bypass normal processes. For instance, an ADM might be asked to draft a cabinet report overnight, without the ability to access guidance from staff. In such circumstances, policy recommendations are made without an awareness of the full scope of risks and benefits.[9] Other cases involve considerable public pressure for the government to resolve individual circumstances, such as a sewer backup that damages basements of uninsured homeowners, or an expensive experimental drug therapy that is potentially lifesaving but is not included in the provincial drug formulary. The public fascination with this single policy issue becomes so intense that the government is unable to advance any issues without journalists pressing for a resolution. To get through this period of intense public pressure, a minister might make a policy announcement that goes against longstanding practices, and is contrary to advice from public servants. This does not necessarily create a precedent. Public policy can be like a rubber band that snaps back into shape once a political crisis is over.

Tip: Practise Real-Time Information Monitoring

Setting up Google alerts for your minister, policy area, or jurisdiction can help you stay abreast of political developments. Considering the constraints on their time, senior-level officials in your organization may appreciate being kept abreast of breaking events.

This way of thinking provides insight into how political cycles overlap with legislative calendars and policy cycles. It allows public servants to be strategic in terms of how and when to pursue innovative approaches to programs and services. Typically it is only in the first two years of a mandate that a governing party is willing to embark on major policy initiatives, particularly on controversial issues. In the final year of a government's mandate, a politically astute bureaucrat knows that ministers are in election mode. Cabinet will prioritize remaining campaign promises and high-profile announcements. New legislative and policy initiatives that fall outside those commitments are less likely to receive attention as the election draws nearer.

Public Policy Lenses

By now it should be clear that policymaking involves the consideration of countless inputs. As mentioned, a mechanism to ensure that important points of view are not overlooked is the formal integration of perspectives in a *memorandum to cabinet* or cabinet report. A cabinet submission is a succinct analysis of a policy issue that recommends a course of action to the executive branch of government. It is typically drafted by policy analysts and reviewed by more senior bureaucrats before being handed off to political staff. Cabinet submissions provide advice to ministers who consider the document's information during cabinet meetings or committees.

The nonpartisan elements of the guidance are based on a review of information and consultations with stakeholders. Good research, strong writing, and attention to presentation detail are essential. Information must be presented in an objective manner. To maximize efficiency and the approvals process, authors of cabinet documents must strictly adhere to a standardized format. If you or your manager liaise with staff in the Privy/Executive Council Office, you might be able to enquire informally about how the cabinet makes decisions, and what public servants can do to better support ministers. What types of extra information are ministers seeking when they return cabinet documents for more work? Do they want more focus on stakeholder views? Are the ministers looking for a gender-based analysis? When asking, keep any questions general. Be sure to respect the chain of command and the professional expectations of your colleagues and superiors.

Each jurisdiction applies its own *policy lenses* to examine the suitability of a proposed policy. The Government of Canada's memoranda require an array of considerations (Table 2). These are subject to change depending on local traditions and which party is in power. For instance, at the provincial and territorial level it is common to apply a rural policy lens. New lenses are added in times of crisis or political change. A health pandemic, economic recession, or security threat will lead to an urgent need to consider all government policy with those priorities in mind. A gender lens no longer treats gender as binary. Governments who take reconciliation and court rulings seriously must ensure that Indigenous perspectives are incorporated into policymaking processes. Politicians and public servants must take these considerations and many more into account.

TABLE 2 Considerations in a Memorandum to Cabinet, Government of Canada

Required Considerations
• privacy impacts
• Official Languages Act requirements
• gender-based analysis

Other Considerations
• legal risk assessment including *Charter of Rights and Freedoms* and trade
• information on any relevant reviews (e.g., Auditor General reports, strategic reviews, internal audits, and program evaluations)
• horizontal policy impacts (e.g., implications for other federal policies)
• sustainable development aspects and results of Strategic Environmental Assessments
• provincial/territorial or regional considerations and strategies, including federal spending power considerations
• private and voluntary sector implications
• international perspectives

Source: Canada, "Memorandum to Cabinet (July 2014)," 2017. Available at https://www.canada.ca/content/dam/pco-bcp/images/pco/mem-cabinet/mc-eng.doc.

Policy lenses matter. They reflect the multidimensional facets of modern governance. They help government departments avoid operating in silos and inhibit the potential for advancing policy with unintended implications. Internal and external consultation with other applicable government units and stakeholders is essential. Accountability functions (see **Chapter 4**) must be contemplated, such as the findings of the auditor general. These are just some of the numerous formal policy lenses.

In addition, there are multiple informal lenses that are applied to ensure congruence with the governing party and its leader. These are intuitive and require some *political acumen* (discussed in **Chapter 5**). Policy proposals that conflict with the values and public image of a prime minister or premier are unlikely to advance. Conversely, a policy that delivers on the governing party's commitments is likely to progress. A promise made on the campaign trail that then appears in the party's election platform, is articulated in a ministerial mandate letter, is mentioned in the speech from the throne, and is allocated money in the government budget is clearly a priority. Other pledges and issues receive little attention, perhaps signalling that the government has changed its policy direction. After all, public policy is whatever a government chooses to do or not to do.

Chapter Takeaways

This chapter illustrates that public servants must be attuned to the politics of the policymaking process.

- Policy involves the translation of power into action. Understanding the power dynamics within the broader political system is a prerequisite for identifying and resolving policy problems.
- The policy cycle is a general guide for understanding how policy is developed and implemented. A more accurate picture emerges when you consider how seldom your work conforms to these categories. Public servants should strive to guide the process back in line.
- Public servants must be attuned to the political rhythms of their jurisdiction. Election cycles, in particular, have fast and slow periods when it comes to the development of new policy directions.
- Policymakers consider a wide array of information when making decisions. Only a fraction of this comes from public servants. Political decisions therefore may or may not align with the advice provided in briefing notes or cabinet documents.

Notes

1   Quoted in Givetash and Smart (2018).
2   Dye (1978), 3.
3   Simon (2007), 1.
4   Howlett, Ramesh, and Perl (2009), 141.

5   For more information, see Howlett (2002).

6   Chase (2011).

7   For more, see Waterman and Meier (1998).

8   Howlett, Ramesh, and Perl (2009), 191.

9   Mucciaroni (2013).

CHAPTER 4

THE POLITICS OF PUBLIC ADMINISTRATION

There are many pathways to a government job. Suppose Angela applies for a publicly advertised position. She needs to submit a detailed application that passes through screening criteria. In one or more interviews, and perhaps a written test, she needs to convince a hiring committee that she has the knowledge, skills, and abilities to perform the advertised duties. Other jobs are posted online exclusively for existing employees. Internal job competitions are how people like Bohdi move around from job to job, occasionally up the organizational ladder. The rules-based nature of the hiring process helps to ensure that Angela and Bohdi are hired on merit, irrespective of their relationships with hiring managers. By comparison, political positions are temporary and are filled using loyalty-based criteria as well as merit. Chris might be hired on as a political staffer with barely an interview on the basis of being a candidate in the previous election or his family's connections with the governing party. He is not subject to the same codes of behaviour as public servants and nevertheless may be eligible to apply for internal public service jobs.[1] How Angela, Bohdi, and Chris were hired matters little when they are thrust together to implement directives from the minister's office. What matters is that they recognize each of them performs an important role. Even the most apolitical of public servants must be attuned to these sorts of internal (small p) political realities.

Our opening chapters established the basic tenets of politics and governance in Canada. For the most part, however, the Canadian constitution and the laws that flow from it do not dictate precisely how various political actors should behave within the system. Rather, they act as guideposts between which citizens, activists, bureaucrats, journalists, legislators, Indigenous leaders, first ministers, and others must operate. This chapter explores the space between those guideposts. It reveals just how murky the rules of public administration can be.

Accountability

Delivering on a government's agenda requires a firm sense of who is accountable to whom, for what. In **Chapter 2**, we discussed how responsible government holds cabinet accountable to the legislature through the concept of confidence. We mentioned that individual ministers are held accountable to the rest of cabinet for delivering on agreed-upon priorities. In addition, Canada's form of representative democracy holds individual legislators accountable to their constituents through elections. Furthermore, party leaders are held to account by caucus and party members, and by their opponents. Voters pass judgment on governments and politicians through these indirect ways.

Accountability is a more complicated concept within the bureaucracy itself.[2] In a strict sense, accountability ought to be confined to the relationship between ministers and the legislature. In a broader sense, a large number of public service organizations have adopted the term as one of their core ethical principles (see **Chapter 5**).

Ask public servants to whom they are accountable and you are likely to hear a range of responses. Some may reply that they work for their respective ministers. Others view their relationship with their direct supervisors as taking precedence. Some believe they are employed by taxpayers or citizens because the title of their vocation implies serving the public. Still others maintain they report to the premier or prime minister or perhaps the monarch, considering that some jurisdictions require bureaucrats to sign an oath to the Crown. Ultimately, all of these answers are valid. The broad concept of accountability requires public servants to balance their responsibilities according to their own sense of priorities and ethics.

This said, there is a distinction between the concepts of accountability and answerability. Accountability requires ministers and public servants to carry out responsibilities they are assigned by law or policy. Otherwise they face personal or professional consequences. The principle of ministerial responsibility is grounded in this notion of accountability. On the other hand, answerability involves "a duty to inform and explain, but does not include the personal consequences associated with accountability."[3] In this sense, public servants are held directly responsible for poor performance and negligence through disciplinary mechanisms. Deputy ministers may be called to testify before parliamentary committees to answer for the goings-on in their departments. However, it is the minister who is accountable to both the first minister and the legislature for the ministry's performance.

Fortunately, in most instances the interests of all of these actors align. This is not always the case. Public servants may disagree with the government's direction. They may report their disagreement to their supervisors who may, in turn, provide advice up the chain of command to the minister. Some ministers seldom change their minds, particularly on public commitments. This leaves the public servant to choose between implementing the direction or, if they cannot bear to proceed with the direction, finding other courses of action. Without question, loyal implementation is the expectation, except in instances when a law is broken.

What recourse do public servants have when they fundamentally disagree with a political decision? They may request a reassignment to another file or position. What if they suspect wrongdoing that, if disclosed, would undermine the public's confidence in the integrity of government? The alleged wrongdoing should be confirmed by identifying which codes or laws have been broken. A public servant who is worried about personal repercussions of speaking up will stay silent. One who is protected by whistle-blower legislation will have greater confidence to report the inappropriate action to an independent officer of the legislature to investigate. Can a public servant refuse to implement the direction? Disobeying a request from an immediate supervisor or failing to carry out a routine job function constitute grounds for disciplinary action. This includes the possibility of being transferred and/or demoted, or a demand to resign or being fired. We explore an example of this in **Chapter 5**.

An extreme option for a disgruntled employee is to leak the alleged transgression to entities outside the public service, such as to a journalist or the government's opposition. Depending on the nature of the leak, this may result in grounds for dismissal, fines, or even criminal charges. At the very least, revealing government information would contravene the *Public Service Act* or equivalent. The rare practice of government leaks highlights the extent to which certain public servants, under certain circumstances, (mis)interpret their responsibility to citizens as paramount. From a less altruistic perspective, leaks may be evidence of unethical and arrogant actions by public servants who substitute their own judgment for that of a democratically elected government. Leaking is an extreme course of action that rarely warrants considering. The day-to-day functioning of government, and Canadians' confidence in it, requires loyalty from the public service.

> **Tip: Recognize Government Expectations of Confidentiality**
> To understand your responsibility to protect government information, consult a code of ethics, and speak with someone in human resources or an ombudsperson (an impartial investigator).

Centralization of Power

The concentration of power in various parts of each public service flows from this concept of accountability. First ministers wield considerable power over their cabinet colleagues. They often informally assemble so-called *kitchen cabinets* of their closest colleagues to define and oversee the government's agenda. As the heads of government, first ministers amass talent in their central agencies and consolidate top staff in political positions within the Premier's Office or Prime Minister's Office. From time to time, former political staff are employed in the nonpartisan centre of government, including the Executive/Privy Council Office and Treasury Board Secretariat.[4] As discussed in **Chapter 1**, the clerk heads the Executive/Privy Council Office and is the highest-ranking public servant. The clerk is the chief deputy minister and provides advice to the first minister. This includes overseeing the cadre of deputy ministers that serve the remaining members of cabinet.

Individual ministers take a comparable approach within their respective domains. Ministers often create similar central bodies within their own departments. Deputy ministers may create policy coordination, human resources, and communications units within departments. This mirrors the central agencies found in Executive/Privy Council Offices.[5] Deputies clarify shifts in the government's agenda and priorities for all employees of the department. They help staff understand how these policy directions align with the departmental mandate and the roles of various employees.

This dual consolidation of power—at the centre of government and at the top of the hierarchy of each department—sets up a system of intragovernmental relations. Elites at the head of their respective organizations coordinate joint business. Ministers interact with each other around the cabinet table and in committees, just as deputy ministers meet regularly to discuss areas of common cause and interest. In Alberta, for example, deputy ministers gather on a biweekly basis at a meeting called Deputy Ministers' Council. That council, in turn, has several functional committees devoted to areas such as social or economic policy, as well as human resources. Similar standing and ad hoc cross-government bodies exist at lower levels of the bureaucracy. This often runs parallel to the structure of cabinet committees or responds to specific policy priorities.

In this sense, public servants may view the consolidation of power within the bureaucracy through two overlapping lenses. They see that control over the government agenda is concentrated in the centre of government. Control over their minister's agenda is similarly concentrated within their own minister's and deputy minister's offices. Within this system a public servant's ability to influence directions and outcomes is constrained. Supervisors have limited capacity or authority to share information or to communicate advice both up and down the hierarchy. The abilities to convey fearless advice while remaining open with staff and to ensure loyal implementation of political decisions are valued in the public service.

Public Administration Is Political

Governing is a political process. In theory the bureaucracy must be independent of the political realm. It must offer impartial advice to the government of the day regardless of the people and party in power. Public servants are expected to present the best available options within the parameters of the elected government's priorities. They must provide the most effective service possible when implementing the government's directions. Public servants are not empowered to substitute their own preferred policies for those of the government, nor should they provide partisan spin to their respective ministers. Rather, they must provide advice that is consistent with available data and the governing principles articulated by the government. Without evidence, the advice borders on partisan hackery; without attention to party objectives, it risks being unresponsive to the directions of a duly elected government.

Public service jobs seldom come with a procedural manual. The work environment is too nebulous and dynamic for that sort of certainty. The most well-versed public servants have a nuanced understanding of the political world. This enables them to craft strategic solutions to the challenges posed by ministers. The bureaucracy may be nonpartisan—but it is not blind to the importance of politics and ideology.

Here, we must recognize the difference between politics and partisanship. Public servants are expected to be nonpartisan while working for government. That is, they should not openly advocate for the interests of a particular political party during their day-to-day work. However, many public servants are expected to be politically astute. They should apply their knowledge of the political environment to provide the best advice and service in the achievement of government goals. People who seek to transition from political staff to public servant must emphasize their skills over their partisan connections.

> **Tip: Use Broad Terms to Describe a Partisan Position on a Public Service Résumé**
>
> Suppose you meet the required skills and experience to apply for an entry-level position within a provincial bureaucracy. But what if you recently worked as a constituency assistant and volunteer with a Member of Parliament who belongs to a different party than the provincial government? Human resources rules prevent discrimination based on partisan affiliation. Managers will look closely at how you frame your experience in your application and in an interview. You would lack political acumen if you proclaim yourself to be a party supporter, irrespective of which party is in power. This lack of sensitivity to the realities of the public service would be a serious impediment. Were you to describe your background in broader terms—for instance, emphasizing the skills and knowledge you built while working in Ottawa or a constituency office—you could get full value for your prior experience without crossing a partisan line.

Bureaucrats need a solid understanding of the political system in which they operate. They must be aware of the institutions of government, the political culture and economy of their jurisdiction, the history of elections, and the evolution of the party system. A read of the politics of public administration encompasses the external environment. This includes how intergovernmental, international, and Indigenous relations affect domestic governance.

Tip: Participate in Public Service Networking Opportunities
Consider joining a public service organization like the Institute of Public Administration of Canada. IPAC and its regional groups host networking events and lifelong learning seminars on topics relevant to public servants.

Furthermore, public servants working in local government must appreciate differences between municipal and federal/provincial governance. In municipalities, public servants may have regular contact with councillors and their political staff.[6] These dynamics present an added challenge to uphold the public sector bargain in smaller governments.

This sort of situational knowledge is a key component of political acumen, as discussed in **Chapter 5**. The public service of most governments offers training in these areas, which are also covered in university courses in political science and public administration, and professional development workshops. In sum, just because public servants are expected to perform their work in a nonpartisan manner does not mean that public administration is devoid of politics.

The Merit Principle

Government hiring managers are tasked with staffing a qualified and competent public service. Modern public services, like those in Canada, recruit nonpartisan employees using the *merit principle*. This means that most government jobs are open to competition. Positions are awarded to the most competent, qualified applicants based on an impartial and transparent set of employment standards and practices. Job competitions are adjudicated by an independent body (e.g., the public service commission) that is insulated from political pressure. The merit principle extends beyond government hiring to include the awarding of government contracts through tendering processes.

That is the ideal. However, there are variations.[7] For one, public sector positions are not always open to the broader public. Governments confine competitions to Canadian citizens or existing public servants, particularly in times of fiscal restraint. Hiring priorities include public servants on a leave of absence or laid off, employees who have been informed that their position will be eliminated, and certain employees who were medically discharged. Hiring managers may craft positions to secure or retain specific individuals, closing off consideration of other qualified applicants. Whether intentional or subconscious, this type of favouritism has advantages such as talent recruitment and retention, and disadvantages such as low morale and lack of new ways of thinking. To further limit bias in hiring, name-blind techniques can be used, whereby the names of candidates are obscured during the screening process.[8]

Second, hiring managers often rely on their sense of how well each candidate would fit into the existing team. Personality, unique qualities and talents, and other intangible attributes can figure into this subjective part of the decision-making process when top candidates are otherwise equal.

Tip: Chat with an HR Manager about Hiring Practices

Many hiring managers are willing to give you an insider's take on the hiring process. Consider approaching a human resource professional for more information about recruitment and hiring policies. This is particularly useful if you seek information about a specific field.

Third, the merit principle is only one factor in employment decisions. This is particularly true as you advance higher up the organization and as you move outward to arms-length government bodies. For example, some high-level and central agency appointments are based on perceived loyalty or alignment with the values and priorities of the government of the day. In those instances, the office of a prime minister, premier, or minister may take a hands-on approach to selecting the public servants they trust most to implement the government's agenda. In other circumstances a search prioritizes the ability of a candidate to demonstrate an absence of loyalty to any party and exhibit no predisposition in values. What matters is the individual's reputation for making things happen, getting decisions implemented, and helping a minister navigate the complexities of governing. For these reasons many top public service positions are exempt from rules and legislation governing hiring practices.

This loyalty to the government's cause does not mean being loyal to a specific political party. However, many appointments to *agencies, boards, and commissions (ABCs)* do allow the candidate to be affiliated with a political party. These appointments fall under the category of patronage, an age-old practice that dispenses government positions to party loyalists. Many ABC appointments fall under the authority of cabinet. This is beyond the purview of deputy ministers and public service commissions that are responsible for ensuring transparency and fairness in the hiring process. Instead, ministers and government caucus members are asked to suggest appointees based on partisan or personal connections. Many of these nominations are subject to cabinet approval.

Fourth, public services often pursue employment equity goals. Public sector managers must demonstrate efforts to recruit Canadians from underrepresented groups. This is necessary to build a diverse and representative bureaucracy that resembles the citizenry it serves. The federal *Employment Equity Act* requires that "special measures" be taken to address employment disadvantages and the reasonable "accommodation of differences" of women, people with disabilities, Indigenous people, and members of visible minority communities.[9] Provinces and territories often define similar categories for diversity and inclusion in the public service. These aims are not designed to conflict with the merit principle that the most competent and qualified candidate gets the job.

Canada's employment equity practices differ from the affirmative action found in the United States. There, public sector employers use preferential treatment to meet hard quotas in terms of new hires. In Canada, targets are established and recruitment is broadened. However, for the most part, during the hiring process a candidate's personal characteristics may not be considered. Exceptions involve positions where a person's lived experience brings particular value to the role. For instance, Indigenous people may be considered more favourably for an Indigenous relations position because of their familiarity with cultural and community norms. Other roles may require cultural sensitivity and language proficiency, by virtue of dealing with a particular group of stakeholders or clients.

Evolving rules and norms generally ensure the most competent or qualified individuals are hired into typical bureaucratic positions. But there are exceptions.

The Structure and Machinery of Government

Every government in Canada features three separate branches (executive, legislative, and judicial), a host of ministries, and a stable bureaucracy. However, the notion that there is organizational consistency across the country underestimates the complexity and fluidity of the machinery of government.[10]

No two governments look the same. The structure of government within a single jurisdiction can change rapidly and repeatedly over a short period of time. Changes of government are the most obvious catalysts for restructuring. A new party in power and a new executive are likely to reshape government based on their ideological approach or platform commitments. The first minister and cabinet decide how government should be organized, often with advice from the Privy Council or Executive Council Office. The number and names of ministries vary. For example, parties on the political left are likely to have stand-alone labour ministries, while parties on the political right may roll those functions under economic development. Sometimes a cabinet shuffle shifts ministers to new portfolios and/or ministers are added to or removed from cabinet. Other times, a shuffle involves creating, dissolving, renaming, combining, or splitting ministries. Some of these are given to newly appointed ministers, perhaps promoted from parliamentary secretary.

Premiers and prime ministers make mid-term cabinet shuffles for a variety of reasons. This might include the desire to highlight certain areas of government business, such as creating a department to address a hot-button issue or appointing a talented minister to lead a difficult file. There may be the necessity of maintaining the balance of power within the party itself. For this reason, backbenchers are promoted into cabinet or ministers are disciplined for poor performance or lack of loyalty.

Clerks have a different set of considerations when it comes to managing their cadres of deputies. Clerks make recommendations to the first minister about who should be appointed as a deputy minister, decisions that are confirmed by cabinet. Deputy ministers often stay on with their departments to ease the transition of new ministers into their roles following a change in government or cabinet shuffle. After this transition period many DMs are moved to new positions within government. They provide a new lens on a portfolio, bring fresh energy and enthusiasm to their new role, or perhaps have a better personal or professional fit with another minister. Other times they are dismissed from government and thanked for their service. Deputy minister shuffles may occur independently from cabinet shuffles as clerks manage their workforces to implement the government's directions. Shuffles take on different flavours from jurisdiction to jurisdiction. Public servants should be prepared for routine work to slow as new leaders transition into their roles. It is wise during this time to talk to seasoned public servants in your area. Their experiences can provide context for what's to come and the implications for public administration.

After all, that is the purpose of bureaucracies in Canada: to provide nonpartisan advice and service in support of fulfilling the cabinet's agenda. Centralized systems of authority, agenda-setting, human resource management, and accountability exist to facilitate this function. We have explained that these systems do not insulate the public service from the political realm. Indeed, the importance of being politically attuned has never been greater, given that the daily and hourly pressures of the political world have a direct impact on the priorities that define the government's agenda. Thus, bureaucrats operate in a multifaceted world of politics and public administration, requiring a high degree of political acumen and diplomacy.

Chapter Takeaways

This chapter observes that navigating the public service requires an appreciation that public administration is political.

- Public servants may feel conflicting pressures to respond to the demands of different democratic actors—from deputies and non-partisan colleagues to ministers and political staffers to stakeholders and citizens. This is why it is crucial to define and continually re-establish clear lines of accountability.
- The centralization of power in government becomes clear. Agendas are set and policy directives are issued from the centre of each government, and within the centre of each ministry, limiting the ability of rank-and-file public servants to define broad concepts like the public good.
- Public servants are expected to provide expert, professional service in meeting the direction set by government. This is why public servants are hired largely on merit, with provisions designed to ensure the public service broadly reflects the public they serve.
- Governments are prone to reorganize themselves from time to time. This ensures the appropriate leadership and resources are in place to achieve key government priorities.
- It is natural for public servants to feel like movable cogs in an impersonal bureaucratic machine. This feeling should not be confused with dispensability. Public servants play a critical role in ensuring that elected governments fulfil the mandates granted to them by voters.

Notes

1   See, for instance, Brodie (2012) and Shaw (2017).
2   Hurley (2006); Thomas (1998).
3   Privy Council Office (2017).
4   For a profile of political staff, see Wilson (2015).
5   For more on deputy ministers, see Bourgault and Dunn (2014) and Hurley (2006).

6   Sancton (2011), 191–92.

7   Love (1988).

8   Treasury Board of Canada Secretariat (2017).

9   Employment Equity Act, http://laws-lois.justice.gc.ca/eng/acts/E-5.401/
    page-1.html#h-2.

10 For instance, see Johnston (2017).

CHAPTER 5

THE ART OF NAVIGATING LIFE IN GOVERNMENT

Suppose an election is approaching. You really like one political party and its leader more than the others, and you want them to win a majority government. The closer the election gets, the more you cheer for the politician who embodies your personal values, and the more you disdain the alternatives. You exercise your right to vote. You watch intently as news desks project which party is going to form government, which incumbents are re-elected or defeated, and which candidates will serve in the legislature for the first time. Through it all, as a public servant, you keep your opinions to yourself or at least to close company.

During the campaign, some of your government colleagues express their political views. Outside work hours they canvass with a candidate, volunteer in a campaign office, attend political rallies, and post political opinions online. In so doing, those public servants must consider some cardinal rules.[1] One, do not identify yourself as a government employee or disclose information related to your job. Two, avoid commenting on public policies directly related to your position or unit. Three, the higher your rank or public profile, the more cautious you should be. Four, do not engage online using government electronic devices. Finally, practise common sense. The caution from the director general of justice who issued a memo to staff advising "you are a public servant 24/7" must be balanced against the advice of union leaders who encourage employees to exercise their democratic rights.[2]

Whether you choose to be quiet or active in an election campaign, and irrespective of the results on Election Day, a public servant is always expected to loyally serve the government of the day. This presents some tensions. To have a successful career you need the political savvy to know how to navigate the public service, no matter who is in power.

Political Acumen

When most people think of diplomats, they picture high-ranking government representatives on the world stage—ambassadors, secretaries of state, trade negotiators, and the like. These officials share a lot in common with public servants at home. They are astute and agile, prudent and tactful, principled and ethical. They possess what's known as *political acumen* (or acuity), a key element of leadership in the public service.[3] Political acumen encompasses

- broad knowledge of internal and external power structures, both within and across governments;
- refined situational awareness when it comes to the political, economic, and social environment;
- soft skills in diplomacy, including strong emotional and social intelligence, and skills in persuasion and collaborative negotiation; and
- a firm ethical foundation, grounded in the values of the public service.

Political acumen involves an ability to apply knowledge of the political system to work effectively with colleagues, stakeholders, and decision-makers in accomplishing government objectives. It requires understanding the unique and oft-changing interests of ministers and senior bureaucrats, as well as those of various stakeholders and the broader public. It means working with partners across one's own department and in other parts of the bureaucracy to generate consensus around how to advance the government's agenda. Broadly speaking, political acumen amounts to the intersection of four key elements—knowledge of power, situational awareness, soft skills, and ethics of public service—outlined in Figure 6.

Tip: Pay Attention to Your Minister's Social Media Posts

Paying attention to what members of cabinet say on Twitter helps you stay in touch with their political impulses, which may well have an impact on your own work. This situational awareness is critical to developing political acumen.

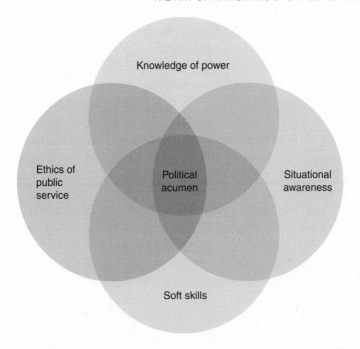

FIGURE 6 Components of Political Acumen

Knowledge of Power

Most public servants know how power is distributed within governments: it is concentrated at the centre of each organization and at the top of the organizational chart. They appreciate that subtle dynamics exist between bureaucrats and their political masters, inside individual ministries, and among different jurisdictions. In other words, they understand the importance of intra- and intergovernmental relations, as well as the international dimension of many policy issues.

In **Chapter 4** we explained the concentration of power in central agencies. Complicating matters, power is distributed among governments in Canada. Very few policy areas are confined to a single jurisdiction. The concentration at the top of each organization helps with coordination, while limiting the influence of any single public servant.

First ministers' meetings sit at the apex of this system. The prime minister speaks and meets with provincial/territorial premiers individually to discuss localized matters. Group meetings are called to generate consensus on pan-Canadian issues like health care and climate change.[4] Premiers meet twice a year without the prime minister, as the Council of the Federation. These forums are an opportunity for collaboration on economic, social, and environmental issues and to pressure the federal government.[5] By far the most visible, these first minister summits are only some of many avenues within Canada's system of intergovernmental bodies.

Federal, provincial, and territorial (FPT) ministers meet regularly with their counterparts to tackle common challenges and share best practices. Separate meetings of justice, health, social services, education, environment, natural resources, finance, and other ministers take place throughout each year. Ministers responsible for Indigenous affairs meet alongside Indigenous leaders in what is known as the Federal Provincial Territorial Indigenous Forum.

An expansive field of bureaucracy has grown within each jurisdiction to support Canada's complex web of intergovernmental relations.[6] Deputy ministers must collaborate to prepare for meetings of premiers and ministers. Below them, public servants hold teleconferences to stay abreast of the goings-on in their policy areas. They recognize that the decisions of one government may impact others. Moreover, governments are often dependent on one another to advance policy agendas. The legalization of cannabis is a good example. Revising the federal *Criminal Code* to legalize possession and recreational use of cannabis has had downstream effects on provincial and territorial governments. Those organizations were required to set up a safe system of distribution, and to address dozens of considerations related to issues such as taxation, public health, and policing. They also had to consider how integrated or harmonized the system would be across provincial and territorial borders, especially in terms of the minimum age of consumption and the tax rate for cannabis. The federal government's timeline provided about a year to pass hundreds of legislative and regulatory changes across the country.

Situational Awareness

Public servants should understand the complex, ever-changing world around them. You must have a good radar to pick up on all of the political, economic, and social influences on your work—and an even better filter to determine the most important pieces of intelligence amid all that information. In other words, you want to catch everything, but be selective in what you retain and use.

As discussed in **Chapter 3**, public servants must be attuned to the political goings-on in their jurisdiction, if only because of how politics impacts the policy cycle and timing of major government initiatives. Politicians may open and close windows of opportunity as quickly as the popularity of governments wax and wane. Public servants need to be attuned to political undercurrents so as to anticipate challenges and tensions, and be responsive at critical times.[7] Advancing some policy files means playing a long game. Periodically the right combination of leadership, resources, and public interest will result in significant progress being made on a particular topic.

> **Tip: Pitch New Ideas When the Timing Is Right**
> Most good ideas don't get shelved; they just await the right opportunity. When the conditions align to advance policy innovation, a public servant needs to be ready with previous studies, evidence, and practical ideas to catch the moment. A prepared public servant can make an enormous contribution at the appropriate time.

Pay attention to multiple sources of media. Being politically aware means more than following opinion polls, reading headlines, or watching question period theatre. Political tremors are much subtler and require ears to the ground. As discussed above, you should pay attention to the power dynamics within governments in order to assess your leaders' room to manoeuvre. A rift between ministers or a chasm between cabinet and the backbench is often weeks old by the time it hits the media. This lag can impact the timing and reception of advice. Political divisions among deputy ministers or other senior bureaucrats are unlikely to surface publicly. Yet, such internal conflict will impact the decision-making calculus further up the hierarchy.

Imagine pitching a cross-ministry initiative and discovering that the two lead deputy ministers work poorly together. Awareness of internal dynamics is why it is helpful to develop informal information networks within your own ministry and across government. If handled ethically—with good intention, solid evidence, and reputable sources— informal political intelligence-gathering can make or break a policy initiative. Dedicating time to read media sources, monitor key opinion leaders on social media, and meet informally with a broad network of colleagues—before, during, or after work hours—is worth the effort.

> **Tip: Use Apps to Monitor Developments**
> Numerous apps are available to aggregate social media and traditional media feeds. This allows you to combine forces with people in your networks to stay on top of key stories and events. Flipboard and Slack are two of the more user-friendly platforms. They are exempt from most government firewalls.

Economic matters are a further consideration. Governments have limited control over the fate of their economies.[8] Thus, a public servant staying abreast of global economic trends is not useful from a utilitarian perspective. That said, economies have a direct impact on government budgets. A downturn typically results in calls for spending restraint. Austerity can vary from funding freezes or cuts, to public servant attrition, even layoffs. Economic upswings or downturns may prompt pressure for increased government spending. A spendthrift administration opens opportunities for new or expanded government programs and services. Either scenario could be a catalyst for public sector innovation, the former driven by efficiency, the latter by enhanced capacity. This is why public servants are wise to brush up on basic macroeconomic theory and the principles of public finance. For instance, the terms *economic, fiscal,* and *financial* are related but not interchangeable. The first refers to jobs, salaries, and overall productivity; the second to the taxing and spending actions of governments; and the third to interest rates and market regulation. Familiarity with economic indicators can be useful for some roles in government.

Finally, be aware of social influences. Many public servants are at least partially motivated by the prospect of improving the lives of current and future generations. Doing so requires an in-depth understanding of the broader population. Staying abreast of demographic trends through Statistics Canada updates is part of this. To frame your work and provide the best advice to policymakers, you should know whether a population is growing or shrinking, aging or getting younger, becoming more or less diverse, and so on. More than this, public servants need to be attuned to the social-cultural trends in society. Generational shifts impact citizens' demands on their government.

Soft Skills

Leveraging knowledge and situational awareness requires a high level of social intelligence and strong soft skills. Hard skills are focused techniques such as effective writing or quantitative analysis that are refined through advanced training. Soft skills encompass communication, teamwork, problem-solving, consensus-building, and other attributes needed for a productive working relationship with co-workers. These talents enable a public servant to interact positively with ministers, deputies, political staff, colleagues, stakeholders, and citizens. Soft skills involve compiling and then applying intelligence about one's social environment. They enable planning and executing an effective strategy to bring others onside, if not on board, with your approach to delivering on the government's direction.

Soft skills are among the more enduring characteristics of a post-secondary education that builds a student's intellectual and social capabilities.[9] Public service commissions and human resource departments are placing increased emphasis on this sort of training, as are many university career centres. Just like effective students, public servants must actively listen, build relationships, show initiative, develop self-awareness, and demonstrate leadership. Those aspiring to be managers need a solid grounding in organizing, directing, managing, and leading teams. This is in addition to experience with financial and project management, innovation, evaluation, and strategic planning. All are crucial for effective public administration.

Not everyone in the public service operates in a co-operative way. Competitiveness and obstruction exist. Public servants are increasingly expected to contribute to a respectful workplace that is devoid of bullying, promotes excellent mental health, and provides a safe environment free from harassment. This concept of collaboration corresponds well with the consensus-building required of many public servants.

Co-operation is a challenging process. Political actors seldom desire the same outcome for the same reasons. Building consensus starts with defining a common set of principles to abide by and objectives to pursue. It proceeds to generating commitments among partners to pursue those outcomes jointly, to the benefit of everyone involved. In this way, consensus is not the same as compromise or concession. It requires more strength, perseverance, and talent to collaborate and reach consensus than it does to compete and achieve accommodation. Finding a collaborative solution might require "growing the pie before you slice it." Rather than settling for a fixed set of resources that must be divided among partners, collaborative negotiation involves everyone co-operating to amass a greater body of resources of value to the group, so that—even when those resources are divided—everyone ends up further ahead.

Ethics of Public Service

It is not enough to know how power works and how to use it. Ethics matter. Without moral moorings, politicians and public servants may be tempted to use their knowledge of power structures and their persuasion skills to take advantage of their privileged role for personal gain.[10] When they do, consequences range from loss of credibility to loss of employment, perhaps even imprisonment. Knowledge and skill without ethics diminishes one's influence. Unprincipled behaviour will earn a reputation for slickness but not acuity, no matter how smart or talented you are. Fortunately, unscrupulous behaviour is rare.

This is why ethics constitute the final component of political acumen. To be great at your job, not just to keep it, you need to abide by the written and unwritten principles of public service. Ethical behaviour is necessary to generate trust among colleagues and superiors to get things done. Combined with knowledge and skill, the accumulation of trust and goodwill forms *political capital*, a type of professional currency that may be spent to achieve particularly challenging objectives. Political capital facilitates smoother personal interaction within the bureaucracy. It should not be used to curry favour with ministers and staffers.

SERVING SERVICE
CREATIVITY COURAGE ACCOUNTABILITY
TEAM INNOVATION
DIVERSITY TEAMWORK
COMPETENCE EXCELLENCE
PUBLIC ACT
EFFICIENCY FAIRNESS PEOPLE
PROFESSIONALISM ONE
RESPECT CITIZENS RESPONSIVENESS COLLABORATION
STEWARDSHIP INTEREST DEMOCRACY
TRUST IMPARTIALITY CURIOSITY
GOOD DEDICATION OTHERS
SKILL PASSION
INTEGRITY

FIGURE 7 Public Sector Values in Canada

Most public service organizations in Canada are guided by written ethics codes. The codes outline organizational values that define the bounds of acceptable behaviour. They are remarkably similar across the country. As a word cloud, Figure 7 illustrates the most common values embedded in codes of ethics from provincial and federal jurisdictions. Quebec is excluded because it does not maintain a publicly available code of ethics for civil servants. The larger the word, the more frequently it appears in such values statements.

Codes of ethics are embedded in each public servant's terms of employment. Acting unethically could therefore result in disciplinary action or termination. Even in the absence of formal sanction, failure to abide by ethical principles will result in a loss of trust from colleagues. Without this credibility, no amount of know-how or talent will help a public servant to succeed in an interconnected and collaborative organization like government.

Confronted with the most difficult ethical dilemmas, however, formal codes of conduct provide only broad guidelines. What if a backbench member of the legislature calls your office to request information about a sensitive internal issue? What do you do when a political staffer asks for a briefing note you are drafting and wants to edit it? What if you are providing support to a minister as part of a travelling delegation, and they insist on taking their formal briefings late in the evening, at the hotel lounge? Beyond applying broad principles such as transparency, honesty, integrity, and the like, public servants must weigh their personal values and professional goals against their legal and constitutional obligations.

The necessity of being guided by a moral compass is particularly true of public servants working in arm's-length government agencies. Those organizations' independence from political interference is strained when politicians opt to undermine or controvert their authority to make decisions. Under such circumstances, public servants face an ethical dilemma over whether to relent to government pressure or pursue a legally mandated course of action. The president of the Canadian Nuclear Safety Commission was fired in 2008 by the federal government when she pushed back on political demands to restart an Ontario nuclear reactor that produces medical isotopes. Her reasoning was that the reactor was undergoing urgent safety maintenance. The head of Statistics Canada faced a similar decision when he resigned in 2010 over a dispute with the federal government about changes to the census. While not the head of an arm's-length agency in that he reported to the minister, he nonetheless experienced an ethical conflict over his duties to fulfil Statistics Canada's legislated obligations. Six years later, the next chief statistician resigned rather than implement the government's centralization of computer services. He saw this directive as an infringement on the operations of the statistics agency. The chief statistician announced his resignation while delivering a speech in Statistics Canada's headquarters in Ottawa. Hundreds of public servants applauded.[11] Thus, two people successively holding the same senior government science position resigned over ethical concerns, one during a Conservative government and the next during a Liberal government. All three of these policy disputes illustrate the supremacy of the cabinet over individual public servants.

Although rare, incidents occur within government departments as well. Controversy occurred over a federal scientist's YouTube protest song, in which he was highly critical of the prime minister.[12] The employee was suspended with pay for breaking his department's values and ethics code. He retired instead of waiting for the outcome of an internal investigation. An Employment Insurance investigator was fired for leaking information to a Montreal newspaper outlining expectations that she achieve monthly savings quotas by denying benefits. She found it difficult to pursue a new career.[13]

Very few public servants confront ethical dilemmas that are so high profile or challenging. These experiences demonstrate that public servants have multiple accountabilities and are not bound to blindly follow the directions of elected leaders. Incidents such as these high-light the extent to which ethical decisions may feel intensely personal and case-sensitive. Public service commissions are meant to apply an objective assessment of which documents, rules, and factors should weigh most heavily. This raises questions about the nature of a public servant's role in balancing what is in the public interest versus what is serving the interest of elected officials who have the legal author-ity to govern.[14] Ultimately, a government employee must recognize the supremacy of the Crown's appointed executive, and accept that person's decisions.

Ethical tensions in the public service are longstanding. A federal task force chaired by deputy minister John Tait in the 1990s explored many of the tensions covered in this book.[15] Public servants reported conflicts between their responsibility to provide stability in programs and services while being accountable for innovative results. They grappled with a desire to serve the public while loyally implementing govern-ment directions that fell short of meeting citizens' needs. They cited downsizing and cutbacks as significant barriers to success. Reading the Tait Report may provide today's public servants with solace that the challenges they face are not unique to their generation. It remains an excellent discussion guide for individuals and teams. This said, the report's lack of firm recommendations is of little comfort to those seek-ing concrete solutions to these ethical tensions. Governments across Canada have developed or refined ethics codes in the decades since the Tait Report. The broad guidelines for behaviour are open to interpre-tation by public sector employees and managers. This ethical ambiguity allows flexibility to address incidents on a case-by-case basis. However, the murkiness can be discomforting for those in the midst of a dilemma.

All of this illustrates that discretion is warranted with respect to loyal implementation. Requests to take action that would go outside of the rules established in law or employment guidelines are prob-lematic. Deleting emails or shredding documents in anticipation of the content being publicly available through access to information is clearly deceptive, for instance. In fact, doing so can result in crimi-nal conviction and imprisonment.[16] Fudging the numbers in a public report is unacceptable. So is hiring someone on the basis of their personal or partisan relationship with the minister. Other situations are muddier. If it is wrong to conduct partisan behaviour, and yet all political decisions are coloured by partisanship, when can we be certain that a directive is excessively partisan? If your minister's office insists you rejig a funding formula to ensure that a specific community, known to be in a swing riding, receives more infrastructure dollars, it should give you reason for pause. Yet a public servant does not have the executive authority to overrule a minister who deploys resources in a manner that smacks of permanent campaigning. What should be done? A simple test is to note whether instructions are contrary to the law. If so, a public servant is obligated not to participate, and must inform a supervisor. If something seems dubious or even unethical, but it is legal, the norm is to faithfully implement the decisions. Exercise caution: request instructions in writing; review your public service code of ethics and values; confer with co-workers and superiors; and anticipate that public servants occupying a higher position will uphold the public service bargain. This requires faith that the system is designed to hold the government accountable. The more challenging path requires you to be familiar with the politics of public policy and public administration. Whatever your position, you retain legal rights and personal moral standards.

You must accept that it is a public servant's responsibility to loyally implement lawful decisions and policies, irrespective of personal feelings. The only practical alternative is to seek a different career.

Chapter Takeaways

This chapter suggests that navigating life in government requires a high degree of political acumen.

- To frame options and recommendations appropriately, you must understand the formal and informal power dynamics within your unit, department, and government.
- Public servants need to be attuned to the world outside their cubicle or office. This situational awareness is key to understanding current challenges and anticipating opportunities to advance your government's agenda.

- Public servants require soft skills to bring people onside with a proposed course of action. Professional development courses can improve your ability to achieve results through people.
- Without an ethical approach you will lack the credibility and political capital necessary to get things done in government.

Notes

1   Public Service Alliance of Canada (2015).

2   Postmedia News (2015).

3   Hartley (2016).

4   Dunn (2016).

5   Simmons (2017).

6   Inwood, Johns, and O'Reilly (2011).

7   Constantinou (2017).

8   Vowles (2016).

9   Axelrod, Anisef, and Lin (2001).

10 See, for example, Greene and Shugarman (2017).

11 *Toronto Star* (2016).

12 Canadian Press (2015).

13 Vincent (2016).

14 For more on this, see Kernaghan and Langford (2014).

15 See Tait (1997).

16 See, for example, CBC News (2018).

CHAPTER 6

ROLES AND COMPETENCIES OF A PUBLIC SERVANT

Public service is a collective endeavour. For better or worse, public servants often strike committees to collaborate. Committees bring together different roles, responsibilities, perspectives, and skill sets. They can be effective forums to brainstorm, plan, implement, and evaluate a specific task. Sometimes committees are highly productive. Participants find synergy and deliver quality work on time. Other committees are filled with tension. A single abrasive personality disrupts an otherwise harmonious work environment; the committee chair's expectations are onerous or nonexistent; meetings are too frequent or infrequent; or perhaps the committee needs management to express a clear will to proceed with a proposed course of action. Chances are that throughout your career you will encounter all of these scenarios, and more. You will need to build and apply your professional competencies to get the most out of these collaborative efforts. There is a vast array of people, roles, and positions in the world of public administration.

Roles and Occupations in the Public Service

When all orders and levels of government are combined, the public service is by far Canada's largest employer. This should not come as a surprise given that government is involved in nearly every part of our lives. Government funds and administers the building and maintenance of roads, hiring and training of teachers, protection of civil rights, regulation of businesses, and care for the sick and the elderly—the list of visible and invisible touchpoints seems never-ending. The resulting scope of roles in the public service is massive, as are the number of employment openings, even in times of fiscal constraint. This broadness can be attractive to aspiring, new, and seasoned public servants alike. There are always opportunities to move among different roles.

Yet it would be folly to consider Canada's public service as a single organization with free-flowing labour mobility. Real barriers confront people seeking to shift jobs between federal, provincial, territorial, and municipal governments. Experience at one level is not always recognized or appreciated at another; the same is true within individual governments. Few behave as a single organization from a human resources perspective. Governments are separated into different ministries, departments, and agencies. Some staff work on the front lines interacting directly with the public while others have desk jobs behind the scenes. Still others work remotely. While most public servants are situated in capital cities, many live and work in other regions. Indeed, of all Government of Canada employees, fewer than half live in the Ottawa capital region.[1]

Where to begin, then, when it comes to understanding where you fit in the public service? There is a detailed recruitment process. Most public service employment sites contain long lists of occupational categories and job classifications. Most offer only a vague sense of what specific jobs entail. The federal government alone lists 30 occupational groups. Within each of these groups are several subcategories.

Comparative analysis across federal and provincial organizations reveals a series of common functional areas in the public service. These are illustrated in Table 3.

TABLE 3 Occupation Areas in the Canadian Public Service

FIELDS	ROLE EXAMPLES
Administrative Support	Clerical, correspondence, data processing
Corporate	Planning, finance, human resources
General Labour/Trades	Maintenance, construction, printing
General Services	Custodial, food services
Operations	Client services, program support, regulation, inspection
Policy	Research, analysis, design
Strategy	Intergovernmental relations, communications
Technical/Professional	Lawyers, social workers, scientists

There are a variety of positions and classifications within each functional area, from entry-level to management. The most high-profile
positions typically reside in policy and strategy. These range from research
or analyst positions in line departments such as health or education, to
policy coordination in the central unit of a department or central agency,
to serving as an executive advisor to a senior or executive manager.

The most numerous and publicly visible roles are in operations.
These include front-line workers delivering programs and services
directly to citizens or stakeholders. Program administrators develop
reports and distribute grants. Regulators and inspectors oversee
program implementation. Technical/professional roles are less visible.
They include legal and scientific advisors, medical services experts,
and others. Arguably the most thankless work lies in the general
services, trades, and administrative support areas. These public servants
provide secretariat, maintenance, facilities, and other forms of support.

A typical department or agency features a full complement of
roles. Indeed, no public service functions effectively without high-
performing staff and solid leadership in all areas. This requires public
servants to develop experience and expertise in particular fields. It used
to be common for employees to spend their entire careers in policy or
operations roles. They would move among different government departments and/or into leadership or management positions within their
field. Today a focus on flow between roles and functions is emerging.

A public service can deliver on policy demands only if there is effective collaboration across these functional areas. Any office worker who
has tried to complete time-sensitive research or correspondence without
access to the Internet can appreciate the importance of IT professionals to
a well-functioning public service. By the same token, strategies and policies must account for the corporate and operational resources required to
deliver on them. Operations and technical/professional work relies on an
appreciation for the intent behind particular policies and strategies.

For these reasons, top public service leaders foster understanding and
collaboration through teamwork. They mobilize groups of public servants
with a variety of functional responsibilities and assign them a common task
or project. Managers aim to provide professional development opportunities for staff willing to transition into new functional areas. Nevertheless,
some of the public service's deepest occupational barriers continue to
separate staff in these various fields, notwithstanding departmental silos.

Tip: Reach Out to Others in Your Field

Feeling trapped in your work? Try engaging with people in your field elsewhere in government to discuss how they developed expertise and job opportunities. These communities of practice make the world of work seem bigger than your cubicle. Networking is a great step toward building a new career path.

It is uncommon to see public servants move across these functional areas. Each field requires unique sets of skills and knowledge. Each often constitutes a separate, insular community with its own unique culture. Stereotypes persist that administrative professionals and technical professionals are not cut out for policy work. Hiring managers in operations might dismiss people with policy and strategy experience as being too distant from the front lines to offer quality service to citizens. There are, no doubt, public servants who have worked their way from the boiler room or mailroom to the boardroom. However, such anecdotes are misleading when it comes to building a realistic career path within the public service (see **Chapter 7**).

An additional consideration is that some public service roles require specialized expertise, credentials, and experience. For instance, deputy attorneys general, who serve their ministers of justice, require legal training. Likewise, nurse consultants who deliver public health initiatives must have applicable credentials. Nonetheless, public services often take a government-wide approach to leadership development and mobility. Ministers and deputy ministers might have backgrounds that are indirectly related to their department. Most senior public servants are expected to spend time in multiple roles in multiple ministries to acquire the skills, knowledge, and networks necessary to support the government's agenda. Early career professionals are encouraged to acquire cross-ministry experience for the same reason.

Building Competencies

Regardless of your career stage, to succeed in government requires the right mix of knowledge, skills, and personal attributes to get the job done. These assets are competencies. They form the basis of public sector recruitment, development, and succession planning in Canada. Governments across the country have remarkably similar competency models. This is reflected in the relative consistency of public service work across Canada. It is complemented by the fact that public service commissions tend to contract the same management consulting firms to help develop and refine models.[2]

What skill sets and abilities are most valued in the public service? Tree maps are a great way to visualize how competency models overlap across jurisdictions. In Figure 8, the more space a term occupies, the more frequently it appears across Canada. Competency models are publicly available for the federal government and all provinces except Quebec and Prince Edward Island. You can consult public service commission or human resources (HR) websites, or contact their HR professionals, to gain access to their respective models. In descending order of importance, governments value seven clusters of competencies among their public servants: the ability to build and maintain relationships among colleagues, clients, partners, and stakeholders; the capacity to achieve results through planning and commitment; strengths across different modes of thinking; leadership capabilities, which are often captured by the notion of political acumen, discussed in **Chapter 5**; effective communication using multiple channels to inform and persuade different audiences; a passion and capacity for self-development; and business-related abilities.

> **Tip: Write Using as Few Words as Possible**
> Public servants must communicate ideas in different formats. Excellent writing skills and presenting information in a concise manner are essential. The ability to conceptualize, design, and use software to translate complex ideas into visual outputs like infographics is a great asset.

Governments place high value on soft skills. Before being hired or promoted, the ideal public servant will possess social and emotional intelligence, and work well with others. Prospective employees are no longer recruited solely because of graduate school credentials and hard skills in quantitative analysis. Existing personnel cannot expect to join the management ranks based solely on subject matter expertise and seniority. Governments insist that public servants demonstrate integrity and ethics, listen actively to colleagues and clients, engage in teamwork, and exude collegiality and inclusiveness. These expectations are outlined in codes of employee behaviour and in learning and development catalogues.

In addition to collaboration skills, governments demand that public servants demonstrate initiative and autonomy in their respective roles. Employees must be agile, resilient, curious, and accountable. Governments often distinguish between employees' capacity to reason in analytical, critical, and systems thinking. This demands that public servants discern trends and patterns, identify process improvements, and position their work in the context of the broader government environment. Other desired competencies include awareness of innovation, long-term thinking, and institutional memory.[3]

> **Tip: Complete Tasks by Their Due Dates**
> Strive to earn a reputation for getting things done and delivering work on time, preferably before deadlines.

For those aspiring to entry-level positions in the public service, the Canadian Association of Programs in Public Administration (CAPPA) identifies the following competencies as crucial prerequisites:

- "the ability to analyze and think critically about public sector problems;
- the ability to lead and manage within public organizations;
- knowledge and understanding of the tools and techniques required to engage stakeholders in policy and governance processes;
- an appreciation of the purpose of public service and associated standards of ethical behaviour;
- a capacity to communicate and interact both professionally and productively with a diverse and changing citizenry."[4]

This is a formidable list of qualities for seasoned public servants to possess. It can be daunting to new professionals looking to advance in their careers. Students and recent graduates seeking an entry-level position in government might worry that they lack appropriate skills, training, and experience. How do you go about measuring and developing your competencies in these areas?

You already possess many of these qualities. It is simply a matter of recognizing and tying them to specific experiences that you have

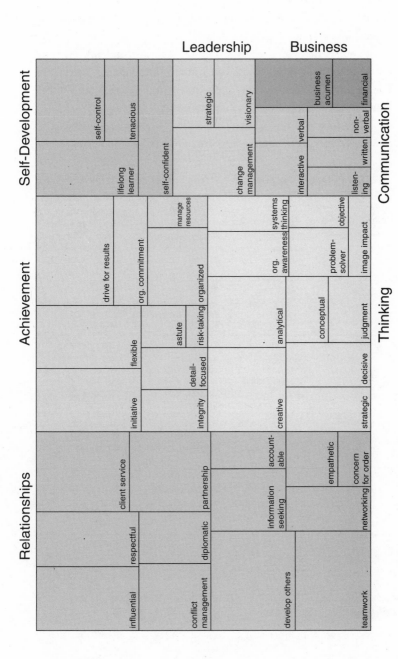

FIGURE 8 Professional Competencies

encountered. Illustrate your competencies by telling stories about how you have applied them. In an interview, public sector employers will express limited interest in your schooling, the professional development courses that you took, or even the positions you held. They are more interested in the lessons you learned (knowledge), the talents you acquired (skills), and the reputation you developed (attributes). This requires a high level of self-awareness.

How do you know where your strengths and weaknesses are in these core competencies? Table 4 contains catalytic questions. Many

TABLE 4 Potential Questions in a Public Sector Job Interview

COMPETENCY	KNOWLEDGE QUESTIONS	SKILLS QUESTIONS	ATTRIBUTES QUESTIONS
Achievement	What did you learn from your last big success? Your last failure?	How have you learned to produce results under stress?	What would your supervisors say about your ability to deliver results?
Business	How do you go about drafting a budget?	When have you had to accomplish more with less, and how did you do it?	What illustrates your commitment to fiscal responsibility?
Communication	What are the biggest barriers to people understanding you?	What's the most you've ever written in the shortest amount of time, and what helped you most?	When did you clearly convey a difficult message, and how did the audience respond?
Leadership	Which leadership model aligns best with your approach?	How have you generated consensus among disparate interests?	What would your followers say about you?
Relationships	Which course, book, or film taught you most about human interaction?	How do you resolve conflict with your supervisors?	What would your peers say about you?
Self-Development	What's the one area you hope to develop through your next work experience?	How do you ensure you learn from your mistakes?	What's the best demonstration of your commitment to lifelong learning?
Thinking	What's your go-to model for problem-solving?	When was the last time you thought quickly on your feet?	How do you ensure your work makes a positive impact on the broader system?

of these are potential questions you might face in a public sector interview. If you have difficulty answering, you may need to develop competency in that area.

To develop your competencies, it helps to discuss your performance with people that you worked most closely with, be they supervisors/instructors, peers/colleagues, or people who you led in team/group situations. Simple questions such as "What is one time you have seen me communicate effectively?" or "What's the single best way for me to improve myself as a team player?" can go a long way toward assessing and improving your competencies. Formal versions of these 360-degree assessments are common development tools within public service organizations. Simple, but frank, discussions over coffee suffice to provide you with feedback to identify strengths, weaknesses, and ways forward. The further that you progress in your career, the more potential information you can glean from these conversations.

Tip: Explore Competency Self-Assessment Tools

Competency assessment tools abound online. Kouzes and Posner's *Leadership Practices Inventory* assessment, Gallup's *StrengthsFinder,* the Thomas-Kilmann *Conflict Mode Inventory*, the University of Victoria's *Core Competencies Self-Assessment Tool,* and others are easily accessible.

Networking is another important component for improving your performance and advancing your career. The adage "It's not what you know, but who you know" extends beyond managers hiring people they met on previous occasions. Recall that in the public service there are rules against those sorts of practices (**Chapter 4**). Building broad and deep networks of public and private sector colleagues holds a number of advantages. Networking demonstrates your capacity for relationship-building and enhances your ability to think systemically. A pre-existing network is seen as an asset and potential resource for prospective employers. This is particularly true in roles involving stake-holder and client engagement. A personal network can alert you to upcoming employment opportunities, allowing you to explore and prepare in advance. Colleagues can provide direct referrals for unad-vertised positions. You can communicate with mentors to provide advice and honest competency assessments that enhance your development. Furthermore, a broad network can allow you to explore different fields of work and to explore your interests.

Relational and Experiential Learning

Another way you can develop competencies is through professional development courses, books, and online resources. While these formal learning opportunities are useful, they are a small part of how we acquire knowledge. It is not enough to rely on courses in political science and public administration.[5] Post-secondary teaching seldom practises skills in real-world contexts or emphasizes career preparation.[6] To round out your development, you should seek out relational and experiential learning opportunities.

Research supporting the value of this sort of multi-modal learning dates back to landmark studies at the Centre for Creative Leadership.[7] The model holds that hands-on experience is the most beneficial for adult learners. Experiential learning involves the application of knowledge and skills, helping to enhance and refine both. Their findings, and those of subsequent studies, suggest that up to 70 percent of what adults learn is through this experiential mode. Another 20 percent is through people, including coaching, mentoring, and peer-to-peer interactions. Knowledge is exchanged and feedback is incorporated to build skills. Experiential and relational learning are most likely to generate the stories and references necessary to succeed in job applications and interviews. The most surprising, and oft-tested, finding from the Centre for Creative Leadership research concerns the notion that 10 percent of learning takes place in formal settings, such as classroom lectures and assigned readings. Given this, *The Public Servant's Guide* will be of greatest value if you supplement it with experiential and people-oriented learning.

Public sector organizations and post-secondary institutions are adapting to multi-modal learning. Human resources professionals within universities have been among the first in the knowledge sector to adopt the 70/20/10 approach to teaching and learning.[8] Yet most academic programming remains focused on formal learning. Public service commissions across Canada have yet to fully embrace the model.

The bulk of their learning and development offerings are confined to in-class and online courses of the passive learning variety. This sort of knowledge mobilization is a key element of succession planning within public sector organizations. However, career development requires a level of prioritization that is sometimes absent in government.[9]

This leaves many emerging and accomplished public servants to find their own relational and experiential learning opportunities. Coaching and mentorship programs exist to link those with more and less public sector experience. Coaches typically offer short-term skill development and career counselling support for a fee. Mentors provide longer-term, more holistic support for professional growth at no cost. Finding the right coach or mentor is a process that involves a combination of referrals and online searches. Being part of a recognized program or having positive references from respected colleagues will go a long way to ensuring a successful relational learning experience.

Genuine experiential learning opportunities are more difficult to come by. University students and recent graduates may take advantage of part-time practicum and internship placements. Co-operative education programs feature full-time, repetitive learning experiences that enable students to build relationships with potential employers (see the related Tip box on the next page). Students in such work-integrated learning programs may be eligible to be "bridged in," a mechanism that allows them to be hired without being subject to the lengthy government hiring process. Secondments, temporary stretch assignments, and cross-department working groups can have a similar impact on early career public servants seeking to expand their networks, knowledge, and skill sets. Formal interchanges with other organizations and task team assignments can do the same for seasoned public servants. These experiential learning opportunities are valuable to those beginning a career. However, they are not a large source of employee recruitment.

Beyond this, people may seek out volunteer opportunities with nonprofit organizations whose work resembles or interacts with the public sector. Serving on a board of directors or volunteering for working committees can provide critical experience with strategy development, project planning, budget management, communications, and teamwork. Such extracurricular activity builds your professional network.

Tips for Concluding a Public Service Work Placement
When a co-operative education placement or internship concludes, a student might want to do the following:

- discuss a job title that represents the placement experience, if one was not assigned;
- write out a job description, if one did not exist;
- send a thank-you letter/card to the workplace supervisor;
- create a list of contacts from the work placement; and
- add content to a career portfolio, including a letter of reference, performance evaluation, brochures, written work, printouts of online contributions, and any other applicable materials to document what work was involved. (Be sure to obtain approvals from the employer as appropriate.)

Table 5 outlines developmental ideas in each of the seven competency areas, including formal, relational, and experiential opportunities. By being purposeful and creating learning opportunities like these, public servants can build a broad repertoire of knowledge, skills, and experiences to support job applications, interviews, and performance reviews. In your own career, you may benefit from documenting the knowledge, skills, and personal attributes you employ or acquire whenever you overcome a challenging situation. Your competency journal will be a useful resource as you prepare for job applications, performance reviews, and promotions.

TABLE 5 Formal (F), Relational (R), and Experiential (E) Learning Opportunities

COMPETENCY CLUSTER	IN SCHOOL	IN A VOLUNTARY ORGANIZATION	IN GOVERNMENT
Achievement	Lead at least one extracurricular project to completion (E)	Assist in the organization's strategic planning (E)	Invite a known innovator to be your mentor (R)
Business	Review literature on public finance (F)	Shadow a treasurer (R)	Debrief with a financial officer after budget season (R)
Communication	Take/teach effective writing clinics (F/R)	Assist with a voluntary organization's social media strategy (E)	Ask to observe verbal briefings with senior personnel/ solicit feedback on your briefings (R)
Leadership	Serve on a student club board (E)	Offer to mentor new members of the voluntary organization (R)	Teach a development course in your area of expertise (F)
Relationships	Select classes with group work (R/E)	Organize networking events (R)	Take social intelligence training (F)
Self-Development	Participate in professional development workshops (F)	Take on new tasks outside your comfort zone to develop resilience (E)	Engage in 360-degree competency assessments (R)
Thinking	Take courses or workshops in systemic design (F)	Identify challenges in common with other voluntary organizations, and partner to solve them (R/E)	Attend/organize cross-government events to develop organizational awareness (R)

Chapter Takeaways

This chapter explains that the varied roles and competencies of a public servant can be both exciting and daunting for early career professionals.

- A wide range of roles exists in the public service. Those with the right competencies, networks, and persistence can navigate a career that spans different sectors, fields, and governments. We discuss this further in **Chapter 7**.
- As the challenges facing governments cut across the same sorts of boundaries, public service leaders expect more from their employees in terms of their ability to communicate and collaborate with colleagues inside and outside government.
- Public servants need self-awareness and a commitment to self-development to build their careers.
- Relational and experiential learning (i.e., working with others in real-world environments) are generally more effective forms of learning than sitting in a classroom or reading.

Notes

1   See Population of the Federal Public Service by Province, https://www.canada.ca/en/treasury-board-secretariat/services/innovation/human-resources-statistics/population-federal-public-service-geographic-region.html.

2   The Philadelphia-based Hay Group, a global management consulting firm, is the most prominent. It has consulted directly on, or influences, more than half of all provincial/territorial competency models.

3   Baskoy, Evans, and Shields (2011).

4   Canadian Association of Programs in Public Administration (2017).

5   Lapointe, Ouimet, Charbonneau, and Beorofei (2015).

6   Collins, Knotts, and Schiff (2012).

7   Lobardo and Eichinger (2010).

8   See, for example, Princeton University (2017).

9   Watts (2000).

CHAPTER 7

ACHIEVING YOUR CAREER GOALS

Most people move from job to job and organization to organization over the course of their working lives. Public servants are insulated from the worst elements of the precarious work economy. Compared with workers in other sectors, they enjoy greater job security, competitive wages, pension plans, insurance benefits including medical and dental coverage, and vacation time. Regular hours rather than shiftwork are another advantage to most public service roles, although work can drift into personal time, as with any job. For those starting out, there are student employment programs and even tuition rebates; for those who climb the ranks there is generous executive pay and benefits. These rewards come with the public service bargain we outlined in **Chapters 1** and **2**.

These privileges notwithstanding, the structure of the public service presents both opportunities and challenges when it comes to career building. As this chapter illustrates, you should avoid thinking about your career in linear terms, and anticipate applying for job opportunities across government. Many public sector career paths are available if you are prepared and equipped to pursue them.

Finding Purpose in a Public Service Career

A good way to prepare to build your career is to discover your broader personal and professional purpose. You need to think beyond any particular job or career objectives. This will keep your expectations in check. Some public servants may be disappointed when their day-to-day work fails to make a difference in society and in the lives of individual citizens. Without a broader sense of purpose, they may feel disgruntled when work stalls amid a cabinet shuffle or gets hung up in committees. Regardless of your commitment to public service, you may feel rudderless when navigating the job boards, or discouraged if you are unsuccessful in successive job applications. Without a grander purpose, you risk losing perspective about how your job fits into your broader life goals and objectives.

There are innumerable ways to define and refine your life's purpose, and your public service career's purpose within it. In some Indigenous cultures, vision quests mark a spiritual rite of passage as teenagers transition to adulthood, requiring participants to define their roles in the community and the best means of serving the people within it. When it comes to finding your professional purpose, the Japanese concept of *ikigai* can be a useful guide. Loosely translated, the term means "your reason for getting up in the morning," or in French, your *raison d'etre*. Finding *ikigai* is a deeply personal and lifelong process, one that involves repeatedly responding to four core sets of questions (Table 6). Your purpose is not found in doing something you are great at, nor is it about achieving a certain social or economic status. It is not about following your bliss or filling a gap in the workforce. Rather, purpose is about building a life that allows you to find gratification on all four levels. Achieving goals in a public service career should bear in mind these core questions.

Consider engaging others in your search for purpose. Frank conversations with close family members, friends, mentors, and colleagues is a

TABLE 6 Core Questions in Finding Purpose

CORE QUESTION	SUBQUESTIONS
1. What do I do well?	What skills or aptitudes do I bring to the organizations and communities I serve? What seems to come naturally to me or can I do without really trying?
2. What do I love to do?	What is the best part of my day? What sort of work do I seem to lose myself in? What gives me energy?
3. What can I get paid to do?	What can I do that helps me provide for my basic needs? What salary level would make me feel that I'm being fairly compensated for my efforts and talents?
4. What does the world need?	How can I contribute most to the world around me? What unique niche can I fill that will improve my community?

good way to supplement your own self-evaluation, as are the 360-degree assessment tools discussed in **Chapter 6**. A life or career coach can offer an outsider's perspective on your situation. Together you can reflect on the many components of purpose, illustrated in Figure 9.

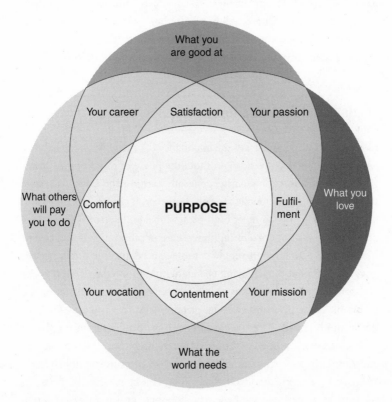

FIGURE 9 Finding Career Purpose
Source: Adapted from Marc Winn, "What Is Your Ikigai?," 2014. Available at http://theviewinside.me/what-is-your-ikigai/.

Answers to career and life questions may well overlap. Yet it is rare that anyone will find a specific public service position that allows them to excel, pursue passions, make a great living, and contribute meaningfully to society all at once. Not everything you are good at is something the world needs, just as not everything you love will generate a source of income. Every job has frustration and boredom. There are crucial ethical and constitutional boundaries when it comes to serving your grander purpose in the public service. As discussed throughout this book, public servants exist to serve government, and it is government that defines the public good.

This is why you should develop a life outside of your job. Cultivate passions through family and friends, hobbies, volunteerism, philanthropy, and so on. There will be days when you feel less competent and even less impactful in your work. Sensing that you are pursuing your grander purpose can help guide you through those low times.

Finding Balance in a Public Service Career

Identifying your purpose raises the importance of finding work-life balance. Many public service positions promote the peace of mind of little stress, good compensation, job security, generous vacation and leave, and stable work hours. For some public servants, however, it can be difficult to find the time and energy to meet both professional and personal goals. This may result in burnout or a diminishing sense of purpose. Few feel able to meet demands of an increasingly complex and expansive public sector, governments bent on achieving change within four-year election cycles and constricting budgets, and 24/7 news cycles and electronic communication. These pressures cascade, placing stress on employees further down the hierarchy. Yet, according to most public sector employee surveys, leaders themselves report relatively high levels of engagement and satisfaction in their work. Their employees demonstrate similar levels of engagement compared to workers in other sectors.[1] This suggests, on the surface at least, that the benefits of a public service career outweigh the costs. Few of these employee surveys tap attitudes beyond the workplace, however. This leaves us to infer the challenges that public servants face as they balance work with a fulfilling life outside the office.

Employees sometimes yearn for more time to devote to pursuits outside work, be they related to family, friends, pets, travel, the arts, sports, hobbies, or other priorities and interests. Leaders and HR professionals respond by offering workplace flexibility. This allows public servants to adapt their schedules or work from home provided that they meet certain performance targets. These part-time, flextime, flexplace solutions appear to meet the demands of today's workers, but the extent to which they solve the underlying needs and challenges is unclear.[2] Early research indicates that such practices are warmly received by employees and employers. Staff feel better able to balance their work and home lives. Employers see an increase in productivity.

Flexwork allows employees to shift their workday hours so that they can schedule their work around their personal circumstances. Flex arrangements help employees attend to personal responsibilities, such as child care obligations and caring for aging family members, attending to health issues and medical appointments, and participating in seasonal hunting and agriculture activities.[3] The Government of Canada has had a flexwork policy since 1999, in response to a changing workforce and to make the government an employer of choice. Other jurisdictions have similar policies. Interest is growing as a response to broader policy objectives, such as traffic congestion and climate change. There are downsides. Negative public optics, instances of misuse, and potential for inequality are among the barriers to workplace flexibility policies.[4] Moreover, some major corporations have reversed their work-from-home policies in response to employee feedback about losing touch with their leaders and co-workers, and with corporate concerns over flagging productivity.[5] A takeaway for public sector organizations is that teamwork is generally easier and more productive when it occurs in person. Anyone who has spent five minutes finessing a five-line email message appreciates the value of having your teammate in the cubicle next to you. Technology has yet to find a better way of building the rapport, trust, and creative environments necessary to drive the innovation demanded of public servants (see **Chapter 6**). Flexwork is not a substitute for in-person collaboration.

> **Tip: Keep Your Emails Short**
> The 3-minute rule is a great productivity tool. If it would take you longer than 3 minutes to write a time-sensitive email, consider walking down the hallway or picking up the phone to talk to your colleague.

So, what lessons can we draw from improved workplace flexibility? Public servants and their organizations benefit most when they can work together and devote their full attention to the work at hand.

The opposite is captured in the concept of presenteeism. This is a situation where employees are physically present at work, but not mentally engaged due to poor health, family issues, or other personal concerns. Providing employees with the time necessary to resolve these personal issues outside of work is preferable to having their minds wander to other priorities while in the workplace. Many public sector unions and public service commissions have leave and flextime policies to accommodate these absences.

Ensuring that you are physically, mentally, and spiritually present at work and at home is ultimately your own responsibility. At home, the task of being present is difficult for those who feel tethered to work by smartphones, tablets, and laptops. Likewise, during work hours some feel the need to constantly check in with family members or monitor social media feeds. Indeed, not unlike their counterparts in other sectors, public servants can feel as if their work and home lives are so fully integrated that they are difficult to define, let alone balance. This, again, is where finding one's *ikigai* is crucial.

Tip: Practise Smartphone Etiquette

Tempted to check your smartphone while at work? Try turning it off until breaks or lunchtime. If you must check it during work hours, do so discreetly, ideally in private. This applies to both personal and work phones.

Your professional and personal purpose can act as a compass. This will lead you through difficult times at work and at home. Purpose presents you with the power to approach career planning with honesty, authenticity, and confidence. It keeps you focused beyond your current or next job toward your broader contribution to your field and society. Your purpose will guide you in a precarious job market and an evolving public sector. Restructuring through layoffs is less frequent than routine government reorganizations and eliminating vacant positions. Most public servants have little, if any, say in where they end up working following personnel and department changes that accompany elections, cabinet shuffles, or budget reductions. These can be unnerving times. Beyond anchoring yourself in your purpose, how do you prepare, if not protect, yourself amid the unsteadiness?

Finding Community in a Public Service Career

It is in a public servant's professional interest to build a network. As mentioned in **Chapter 6**, developing a strong group of colleagues and supporters from within your own team, across government, and in other organizations has many advantages. Your network gives you safe places to vent, confide, boast, and celebrate, depending on the circumstance. This will help you maintain your mental, social, and spiritual health. People in your network are fantastic sources for career intelligence. They can fill you in on potential restructuring or job openings and provide you with frank assessments of the leadership and culture in organizations you might consider joining. Your network can serve as your champion when it comes to applying for jobs or leadership roles. Colleagues can place advance calls to prospective employers and provide written or verbal endorsements during a reference check.

> **Tip: Acknowledge Your Colleagues' Achievements**
> Consider endorsing people in your networks for the competencies you've seen them demonstrate. Endorsements can come as formal reference letters or informal email messages that you can save for your portfolio. Praise on social media, like LinkedIn's endorsement tool, can be effective.

A good place to start building your network is through professional associations. They offer educational events, professional development workshops, social activities, online forums, and other venues to connect public servants. Some governments have their own internal groups. Some groups are devoted to new public servants or new managers. Other opportunities to meet colleagues include learning and development sessions hosted by your department, broader organization, or outside companies. Conferences are an excellent forum to meet clients and learn about their needs. In evaluations of these events, organizers often find that participants value the opportunity to meet other people in similar roles across the organization.

If your organization does not have these types of opportunities, it may be possible to create them. Governments across Canada are rife with grassroots communities of practice around policy, operations, service delivery, systemic design, evaluation, public finance, project management, legislative planning, and executive management. These groups often meet informally over beverages or meals. Others are virtual, such as the Government of Canada's GCTools, among them GCpedia (a wiki workspace), GCconnex (a networking platform for federal public servants), and GCcollab (a networking platform for all public servants, academics, and students).

Outside of government there are opportunities to attend public lectures by scholars and think tanks. You can join private or nonprofit sector organizations in your field. Participating broadens your network to include stakeholders, clients, and academics and opens up new career paths outside the public sector. The Institute of Public Administration of Canada (IPAC) is the country's largest organization devoted to promoting excellence in public administration. IPAC has regional groups across Canada, including most provincial and territorial capitals. It offers events and services to members, exclusive job-board listings, and volunteer and board leadership opportunities.

Public servants might be too busy to participate in these activities. Some assume their supervisors will not give them permission to attend during work hours. The value of investing in your networking boils down to priorities, not time or resources. Time is a fixed commodity for everyone. You choose whether to adjust your priorities to focus on networking and professional development. Few supervisors will deny you opportunities to build your network if they are persuaded this will bring value to your workplace performance. Public service units must be open-minded about developing and implementing policy, or designing and delivering public services. Employees with deep and broad networks are an asset in this environment. Some managers may need a gentle reminder about this. Otherwise, engaging in professional development and network building may come on your own time and dime. Chances are it will be worth the investment.

There are other options. Engagement in online communities is an essential practice for today's public servants. Many governments have social media tools for the use of their employees, such as Yammer or Facebook at Work, or the aforementioned GCTools. Likewise, many communities of practice and professional organizations offer online forums to connect their members. The wider world of social media is another networking tool, one that many public servants are wary of using for professional purposes. Many fear contravening codes of behaviour or government policies by publicly communicating about political and policy issues on Twitter, Facebook, or LinkedIn. These worries have merit. Yet social media platforms are a great source for career intelligence and professional development tips. Using a profile with your own name does not obligate you to post or tweet. Many public servants do not, preferring to simply observe online discussions and follow opinion leaders in their field. Anonymous profiles on Facebook and Twitter may allow you to join conversations, although you can expect your voice to carry less weight.

Developing a solid and positive digital profile is increasingly important. Tips on doing so abound online. While it is a myth that many people are recruited through LinkedIn, particularly in the public sector, your profile can matter in terms of landing your next position. Notwithstanding privacy rules, some government HR professionals and hiring managers look at prospective employees' online presence to identify red flags and positive endorsements. Your featured skills and endorsements section should focus on the core competencies expected of public servants (see **Chapter 6**). Members of your network should be able to vouch for your talents in those areas. Above all, be cognizant of what you post. A positive online reputation is of growing importance if you want to achieve your career goals.

Tip: Manage Your Digital Footprint

You should assume that current and future employers will have access to the messages, photos, and videos that you post in public forums such as Facebook, Instagram, LinkedIn, Pinterest, Twitter, and YouTube. Even conversations that you assume to be private can have implications for your career. Public servants who mistakenly "reply all" or who send a text to the wrong number pay the price for indiscriminate language and commentary. When making a public or even private comment, and with certain behaviours in public, the sagest advice may be to ask yourself: Would I be comfortable if my direct supervisor found out about this activity? Would I want this to appear as a news story or on Twitter? If the answer is maybe, it's best to consult. If it's no, and you value your job, it's best to sit it out.

Whether you are addicted to social media, or avoid it entirely, we hope the preceding pages will help you navigate life in the public service. Our objective was to offer a sampling of how government works and what it takes to build and follow a successful career path in the public sector. We believe that being a public servant is much more than just a job. It is a noble venture—one made even more feasible and rewarding if your professional purpose revolves around concepts like working with others to give back to your community. *The Public Servant's Guide to Government in Canada* is just that: a set of suggestions for how to get the most out of your time in government, however short, long, or episodic it may be.

Chapter Takeaways

This chapter impresses that your career is only one part of your life.

- Public servants should understand their broader interests, objectives, and purpose. This keeps you grounded when confronted with the challenges of public service work.
- Few people find complete fulfilment in their work lives. Many struggle to find their dream job.
- Consider pursuing employment that provides you with the resources (funds, time, energy) to contribute to your broader purpose.
- Keeping your broader purpose in mind helps clarify the lines between work and home life. These lines will become blurry at points in your public service career.
- Public servants should search out likeminded colleagues to build strong and supportive personal and professional networks.

Notes

1   Armstrong and Wright (2016); Psychometrics Canada (2011).
2   Van Dyne, Kossek, and Lobel (2007).
3   Employment and Social Development Canada (2016).
4   Israelson (2017).
5   Useem (2017).

GLOSSARY OF TERMS

Accountability: A line of obligation that establishes which individuals and institutions are responsible for decisions.

Agencies, boards, and commissions (ABCs): Government organizations that operate at arm's length from the government and ministers, such as Crown Corporations.

Agenda setting: Competitive political activities that seek to put policy problems and solutions at the top of a government's list of priorities.

Briefing note: A short written summary that succinctly and objectively informs the reader about an issue.

Cabinet: The prime minister (or premier) and ministers who are granted the constitutional authority to make government decisions on behalf of the Crown.

Centre of government: The nucleus of decision-making among senior government personnel. In the Government of Canada the centre is generally understood to include the Prime Minister's Office, the Privy Council Office, the Department of Finance, and the Treasury Board Secretariat.

Clerk: The chief deputy minister and highest-ranking public servant. In the Government of Canada this person heads up the Privy Council Office in Ottawa and serves as Secretary to Cabinet.

Crown: A term that encompasses the regal authority of the monarch as head of state and all branches of government.

Democracy: The use of a free and fair election process for citizens to elect representatives who will represent their interests and oversee government.

Deputy minister (DM): A public servant who is the senior leader of a government department and who serves at the pleasure of the government of the day.

Federalism: A system of government whereby powers and responsibilities are constitutionally assigned to different orders of government, which cannot abrogate each other's areas of jurisdiction.

First minister: The prime minister or premier.

Governor General: The primary representative of the King or Queen of Canada. Exercises constitutional authorities such as appointing a federal cabinet, signing federal bills into law, and authorizing a federal election.

Ikigai: The Japanese concept of a person's reason for being.

Kitchen cabinet: An unofficial term that refers to the main power brokers within a cabinet who oversee key portfolios and are part of the first minister's inner circle. Also known as an inner cabinet.

Lieutenant Governor: In each province, a representative of the King or Queen of Canada. He or she is appointed by the Governor General on advice of the prime minister and federal cabinet, and likewise appoints a provincial cabinet, signs provincial bills into law, and authorizes a provincial election. In the territories similar roles are fulfilled by commissioners.

Majority government: The common situation in which the governing party controls more than half of the seats in the legislature. Thus bills will all but assuredly be passed.

Memorandum to cabinet: A succinct analysis of a policy issue prepared by public servants that recommends a course of action to the executive branch of government. Also known as an MC or a cabinet report.

Merit principle: The standard that public servants must be hired through an advertised formal job competition and on the basis of their competencies.

Minister: A member of the governing party who is appointed to cabinet and is responsible for overseeing a department and/or a government agency or other portfolio.

Minority government: The situation in which members of opposition parties outnumber those of the governing party in the legislature. Since bills are subject to defeat, there is an onus on the governing party to consider the views of members of other parties.

New Political Governance (NPG): A theory that government is becoming politicized.

New Public Management (NPM): A theory that government is adopting businesslike management principles.

Parliamentary secretary: A parliamentarian who has designated responsibilities to assist a minister but is not a member of cabinet. Also known as an associate minister.

Permanent campaigning: The exploitation of public resources for campaign-like use by those in positions of political power.

Policy lenses: The application of varied perspectives to a policy to ensure that important points of view are considered.

Political acumen: The ability to work effectively by applying knowledge of the political, economic, and organizational context, deft social skills, and ethics to achieve government objectives.

Political capital: The accumulation of trust and goodwill that can be used to influence other political actors to achieve desired ends.

Political staff: Impermanent, partisan political appointees who serve at the pleasure of the minister in whose office they are employed.

Premier: The head of a provincial or territorial cabinet and the leader of the political party that controls the legislature.

Premier's Office: The central office in a provincial government that houses the premier and senior political staff.

Prime minister: The head of the federal cabinet and the leader of the political party that controls the House of Commons.

Prime Minister's Office (PMO): The central office in the Government of Canada that houses the prime minister's most senior political advisors, such as the chief of staff, principal secretary, and director of communications, among others.

Principal-agent problem: The concept that policy is not implemented the way that a decision-maker (the principal) originally envisioned because so many public servants and political staff (the agents) provided input during its development.

Privy Council Office (PCO): The central agency in Ottawa that consists of public servants, including the clerk, and operates as the bureaucratic, nonpartisan counterpart to the Prime Minister's Office. The provincial-level equivalent is often known as the Executive Council Office or Cabinet Office.

Public administration: The machinery of government that designs, delivers, and monitors public policies and services.

Public policy: Government decisions and non-decisions that address public problems through rules and the allocation of resources.

Public servants: Permanent employees of government, most of whom are hired based on the merit principle and possess specialized expertise. Otherwise known as bureaucrats and civil servants.

Public service bargain: The idea that the public service serves the needs of their political masters while upholding professional standards and staying out of the public eye.

Truth and Reconciliation Commission of Canada: A federal government commission that from 2008 to 2015 investigated the harms on Indigenous peoples incurred by the Indian residential school system. It issued 94 calls to action for repairing the relationship between Indigenous and non-Indigenous people in Canada.

Weberian bureaucracy: The principle that a public service must feature the common characteristics of an organizational hierarchy, specialized labour, impersonal processes, standardized employment practices, and job security.

REFERENCES

Armstrong, Todd, and Ruth Wright. 2016. "Employee Engagement: Leveraging the Science to Inspire Great Performance." Ottawa: Conference Board of Canada. http://www.conferenceboard.ca/e-library/abstract.aspx?did=7924.

Aucoin, Peter. 1995. *The New Public Management: Canada in Comparative Perspective*. Montreal: Institute for Research on Public Policy.

———. 2012. "New Political Governance in Westminster Systems: Impartial Public Administration and Management Performance at Risk." *Governance: An International Journal of Policy, Administration and Institutions* 25, no. 2: 177–99. https://doi.org/10.1111/j.1468-0491.2012.01569.x.

Axelrod, Paul, Paul Anisef, and Zeng Lin. 2001. "Against All Odds? The Enduring Value of Liberal Education in Universities, Professions, and the Labour Market." *Canadian Journal of Higher Education* 31, no. 2: 47–77.

Baskoy, Tuna, Bryan Evans, and John Shields. 2011. "Assessing Policy Capacity in Canada's Public Services: Perspectives of Deputy and Assistant Deputy Ministers." *Canadian Public Administration* 54, no. 2: 217–34. https://doi.org/10.1111/j.1754-7121.2011.00171.x.

Bourgault, Jacques, and Christopher Dunn, eds. 2014. *Deputy Ministers in Canada: Comparative and Jurisdictional Perspectives*. Toronto: University of Toronto Press.

Brodie, Ian. 2012. "In Defence of Political Staff." *Canadian Parliamentary Review* 35, no. 3: 33–9.

Butterfield, Michelle. 2017. "Canada's Smallest Town, Tilt Cove, N.L., Has a Population of 4." *Huffington Post*, February 17. https://www.huffingtonpost.ca/2017/02/17/tilt-cove-newfoundland_n_14824800.html.

Cabinet Office. 2010. "Template Policy Paper." Department of the Prime Minister and Cabinet, Government of New Zealand. https://www.dpmc.govt.nz/sites/default/files/2017-03/Template-Policy-Paper-02.docx.

Canada. 2017. "Guidance for Deputy Ministers." https://www.canada.ca/en/privy-council/services/publications/guidance-deputy-ministers.html.

Canadian Association of Programs in Public Administration. 2017. "Accreditation." https://cappa.ca/what-we-do/accreditation/.

Canadian Press. 2015. "'Harperman' Federal Scientist Tony Turner Retires Rather than Wait Out Investigation." CBC, October 2. http://www.cbc.ca/news/canada/ottawa/harperman-retires-1.3254757.

CBC News. 2018. "Former Top Ontario Liberal Aide Sentenced to 4 Months in Jail for Role in Gas Plants Scandal." April 10. http://www.cbc.ca/news/canada/toronto/david-livingston-liberal-aid-jail-gas-plants-dalton-mcguinty-1.4613731.

Chase, Steven. 2011. "Government Policy Decisions, in 140 Characters or Less." *The Globe and Mail*, February 3. https://www.theglobeandmail.com/news/politics/government-policy-decisions-in-140-characters-or-less/article564885/.

Collins, Todd A., H. Gibbs Knotts, and Jen Schiff. 2012. "Career Preparation and the Political Science Major: Evidence from Departments." *PS, Political Science & Politics* 45, no. 1: 87–92. https://doi.org/10.1017/S1049096511001764.

Constantinou, Peter. 2017. "Political Acuity and Staff-Council Relations." *Canadian Journal of Local Government* (November): 1–17.

Coulthard, Glen. 2014. *Red Skin, White Masks: Rejecting the Colonial Politics of Recognition*. Minneapolis: University of Minnesota Press, 2014. https://doi.org/10.5749/minnesota/9780816679645.001.0001.

Dunn, Christopher. 2016. "Harper without Jeers, Trudeau without Cheers: Assessing 10 Years of Intergovernmental Relations." *IRPP Insight* no. 8: 1–30.

Dye, Thomas. 1978. *Understanding Public Policy*. 3rd ed. Englewood Cliffs, NJ: Prentice-Hall.

Employment and Social Development Canada. 2016. "Flexible Work Arrangements: What Was Heard." https://www.canada.ca/en/employment-social-development/services/consultations/what-was-heard.html.

Forsey, Eugene. 2005. *How Canadians Govern Themselves*. 6th ed. Ottawa: Library of Parliament. https://lop.parl.ca/About/Parliament/SenatorEugeneForsey/book/assets/pdf/How_Canadians_Govern_Themselves9.pdf.

Gingras, Anne-Marie. 2012. "Access to Information: An Asset for Democracy or Ammunition for Political Conflict, or Both?" *Canadian Public Administration* 55, no. 2: 221–46. https://doi.org/10.1111/j.1754-7121.2012.00215.x.

Givetash, Linda, and Amy Smart. 2018. "Anti-Pipeline Protesters Crash Trudeau's Vancouver Visit." *BNN*, April 5. https://www.bnnbloomberg.ca/energy-environment-to-be-focus-of-trudeau-s-western-canada-trip-1.1047523.

Greene, Ian, and David P. Shugarman, eds. 2017. *Honest Politics Now: What Ethical Conduct Means in Canadian Public Life*. Toronto: James Lorimer & Company.

Hartley, Jean. 2016. "Politics and Political Astuteness in Leadership." In *The Routledge Companion to Leadership*, ed. John Stoney, Jean Hartley, Jean-Louis Denis, et al., 197–208. New York: Taylor & Francis.

Hiebert, Janet. 2002. *Charter Conflicts: What Is Parliament's Role?* Montreal, Kingston: McGill-Queens University Press.

Himelfarb, Alex. 2002. "The Intermestic Challenge." Speaking notes for an address to APEX Symposium 2002. http://www.pco-bcp.gc.ca/index. asp?lang=eng&page=clerk-greffier&sub=archives&doc=20020605-eng.htm. (This material has since been removed from the pco-bcp.gc.ca website.)

Hogan, Michael. 2016. "The 10 Funniest Ever *Yes Minister* Moments." *The Telegraph*, August 24. https://www.telegraph.co.uk/tv/0/ the-10-funniest-ever-yes-minister-moments/.

Hood, Christopher, and Ruth Dixon. 2015. *A Government That Worked Better and Cost Less? Evaluating Three Decades of Reform and Change in UK Central Government.* Oxford: Oxford University Press. https://doi.org/10.1093/ acprof:oso/9780199687022.001.0001.

Howlett, Michael. 2002. "Policy Development." In *The Handbook of Public Administration*, ed. Christopher Dunn, 173–91. Don Mills, ON: Oxford University Press.

Howlett, Michael, M. Ramesh, and Anthony Perl. 2009. *Studying Public Policy: Policy Cycles and Policy Subsystems.* 3rd ed. Don Mills, ON: Oxford University Press.

Hurley, James Ross. 2006. "Responsibility, Accountability, and the Role of Deputy Ministers in the Government of Canada." In *Restoring Accountability: Research Studies, Volume 3—Linkages: Responsibilities and Accountabilities*, ed. Canada, Commission of Inquiry into the Sponsorship Program and Advertising Activities (Gomery Commission). Ottawa: Public Works and Government Services Canada.

InCiSE. 2017. "2017 International Civil Service Effectiveness (InCiSE) Index." https://www.instituteforgovernment.org.uk/publications/ international-civil-service-effectiveness-incise-index-2017.

Inwood, Gregory J., Carolyn M. Johns, and Patricia L. O'Reilly. 2011. *Intergovernmental Policy Capacity in Canada: Inside the Worlds of Finance, Environment, Trade, and Health.* Montreal: McGill-Queen's University Press.

Israelson, Daniel. 2017. "As Government Telework Expands, Things to Consider." *The Globe and Mail*, March 26. https://www. theglobeandmail.com/report-on-business/careers/the-future-of-work/ as-government-telework-expands-things-to-consider/article7981287/.

Johnston, David. 2017. *Thinking Government: Public Administration and Politics in Canada.* 4th ed. Toronto: University of Toronto Press.

Kernaghan, Kenneth, and John Langford. 2014. *The Responsible Public Servant.* 2nd ed. Toronto: Institute of Public Administration of Canada.

Kouzes, James M., and Barry Z. Posner. 2017. *The Leadership Challenge: How to Make Extraordinary Things Happen in Organizations*. 6th ed. Hoboken, NJ: Jossey-Bass.

Lapointe, Luc, Mathieu Ouimet, Marissa Charbonneau, et al. 2015. "Do Canadian University Students in Political Science and Public Administration Learn to Perform Critical Appraisal?" *Canadian Public Administration* 58, no. 3: 487–503. https://doi.org/10.1111/capa.12124.

Lobardo, Michael M., and Robert W. Eichinger. 2010. *Career Architect Development Planner*. 5th ed. Minneapolis, MN: Lominger.

Love, J.D. 1988. "The Merit Principle in the Provincial Governments of Atlantic Canada." *Canadian Public Administration* 31, no. 3: 335–51. https://doi.org/10.1111/j.1754-7121.1988.tb01321.x.

MacDonald, David. 2015. "Five Reasons the TRC Chose 'Cultural Genocide.'" *The Globe and Mail*, July 6. https://www.theglobeandmail.com/opinion/five-reasons-the-trc-chose-cultural-genocide/article25311423/.

Marland, Alex, Thierry Giasson, and Anna Esselment, eds. 2017. *Permanent Campaigning in Canada*. Vancouver: UBC Press.

Mucciaroni, Gary. 2013. "The Garbage Can Model and the Study of the Policy-Making Process." In *Routledge Handbook of Public Policy*, ed. Eduardo Araral Jr., Scott Fritzen, Michael Howlett, M. Ramesh and Xun Wu, 320–8. Abingdon, UK: Routledge.

Mueller, John. 1999. *Capitalism, Democracy, and Ralph's Pretty Good Grocery*. Princeton: Princeton University Press.

Postmedia News. 2015. "'You Are a Public Servant 24/7': Memo Tells Public Servants to Zip It on Social Media during Campaign." *National Post*, August 18. https://nationalpost.com/news/politics/you-are-a-public-servant-247-memo-tells-public-servants-to-zip-it-on-social-media-during-campaign.

Princeton University. 2017. "Learning Philosophy." https://www.princeton.edu/hr/learning/philosophy.

Privy Council Office. 2013. *Blueprint 2020: Building Tomorrow's Public Service Together*. Government of Canada. http://publications.gc.ca/collections/collection_2015/bcp-pco/CP22-101-2013-eng.pdf.

———. 2017. *Guidance for Deputy Ministers*. Government of Canada. https://www.canada.ca/en/privy-council/services/publications/guidance-deputy-ministers.html.

Psychometrics Canada. 2011. *Control, Opportunity and Leadership: A Study of Employee Engagement in the Canadian Workforce*. https://www.psychometrics.com/wp-content/uploads/2015/04/engagement_study.pdf.

Public Service Alliance of Canada. 2015. "Expressing Political Opinions on Social Media: Your Rights." http://psacunion.ca/expressing-political-opinions-social-media-your.

Russell, Peter H. 2008. *Two Cheers for Minority Government: The Evolution of Canadian Parliamentary Democracy.* Toronto: Emond Montgomery.

Sancton, Andrew. 2011. *Canadian Local Government: An Urban Perspective.* Don Mills, ON: Oxford University Press.

Savard, Jean-François, and Christiane Melançon. 2014. "Governmental Priorities and Administrative Rhetoric: The Case of Briefing Notes." In *Canadian Public Administration in the 21st Century*, ed. Charles Conteh and Ian Roberge, 157–72. Boca Raton, FL: CRC Press.

Savoie, Donald. 1999. *Governing from the Centre: The Concentration of Power in Canadian Politics.* Toronto: University of Toronto Press.

———. 2003. *Breaking the Bargain: Public Servants, Ministers, and Parliament.* Toronto: University of Toronto Press.

Schaffer, Bernard. 1973. *The Administrative Factor.* London, UK: Frank Cass.

Shaw, Rob. 2017. "NDP Government Stacks Jobs with Partisan Insiders." *Vancouver Sun*, September 27. http://vancouversun.com/news/politics/ndp-government-stacks-jobs-with-partisan-insiders.

Simmons, Julie M. 2017. "Canadian Multilateral Intergovernmental Institutions and the Limits of Institutional Innovation." *Regional & Federal Studies* 27, no. 5: 573–96. https://doi.org/10.1080/13597566.2017.1389725.

Simon, Christopher A. 2007. *Public Policy: Preferences and Outcomes.* New York: Pearson Education.

Smith, David E. 2013. *The Invisible Crown: The First Principle of Canadian Government.* Toronto: University of Toronto Press.

Statistics Canada. 2012. "Public Sector Employment, Wages and Salaries, by Province and Territory." CANSIM, table 183–0002. http://www.statcan.gc.ca/tables-tableaux/sum-som/l01/cst01/govt62a-eng.htm.

Tait, John. 1997. "A Strong Foundation: Report of the Task Force on Public Service Values and Ethics (the Summary)." *Canadian Public Administration* 40, no. 1: 1–22.

Thomas, Paul G. 1998. "The Changing Nature of Accountability." In *Taking Stock: Assessing Public Sector Reforms*, ed. P. Guy Peters and Donald Savoie, 348–93. Montreal: McGill-Queen's University Press.

Toronto Star. 2016. "Former Chief Statistician's Stand Raises Troubling Questions." Editorial, September 26. https://www.thestar.com/opinion/editorials/2016/09/26/former-chief-statisticians-stand-raises-troubling-questions-editorial.html.

Treasury Board of Canada Secretariat. 2017. "What's in a Name? Name-Blind Recruitment Comes to the Government of Canada." News release, April 20. https://www.canada.ca/en/treasury-board-secretariat/news/2017/04/what_s_in_a_namename-blindrecruitmentcomestothegovernmentofcanad.html.

Truth and Reconciliation Canada. 2015. *Honouring the Truth, Reconciling the Future: Summary of the Final Report of the Truth and Reconciliation Commission of Canada.* Winnipeg: Truth and Reconciliation Commission of Canada.

Udy, Stanley H. 1959. "'Bureaucracy' and 'Rationality' in Weber's Organization Theory: An Empirical Study." *American Sociological Review* 24, no. 6: 791–5. https://doi.org/10.2307/2088566.

Useem, Jerry. 2017. "When Working from Home Doesn't Work." *The Atlantic,* November. https://www.theatlantic.com/magazine/archive/2017/11/when-working-from-home-doesnt-work/540660/.

Van Dyne, Linn, Ellen Kossek, and Sharon Lobel. 2007. "Less Need to Be There: Cross-Level Effects of Work Practices That Support Work-Life Flexibility and Enhance Group Processes and Group-Level OCB." *Human Relations* 60, no. 8: 1123–54. https://doi.org/10.1177/0018726707081657.

Vincent, Donovan. 2016. "Employment Insurance Whistleblower Still Seeking Justice Three Years Later." *Toronto Star,* January 31. https://www.thestar.com/news/insight/2016/01/31/employment-insurance-whistleblower-still-seeking-justice-three-years-later.html.

Vowles, Jack. 2016. "Globalization, Government Debt, Government Agency, and Political Efficacy." In *Globalization and Domestic Politics: Parties, Elections, and Public Opinion,* ed. Jack Vowles and Georgios Zenezonakis, 155–72. Oxford: Oxford University Press. https://doi.org/10.1093/acprof:oso/9780198757986.003.0008.

Waterman, Richard W., and Kenneth J. Meier. 1998. "Principal-Agent Models: An Expansion?" *Journal of Public Administration: Research and Theory* 8, no. 2: 173–202. https://doi.org/10.1093/oxfordjournals.jpart.a024377.

Watts, A.G. 2000. "Career Development and Public Policy." *Journal of Employment Counseling* 37, no. 2: 62–75. https://doi.org/10.1002/j.2161-1920.2000.tb00824.x.

Wesley, Jared. 2017. "Landing Your First Public Sector Job." *Praxis: The CPSA Career Blog,* October 3. http://praxispolisci.ca/landing-your-first-public-sector-job/.

Wilson, R. Paul. 2015. "A Profile of Ministerial Policy Staff in the Government of Canada." *Canadian Journal of Political Science* 48, no. 2: 455–71. https://doi.org/10.1017/S0008423915000293.

———. 2016. "Trust but Verify: Ministerial Policy Advisors and Public Servants in the Government of Canada." *Canadian Public Administration* 59, no. 3: 337–56. https://doi.org/10.1111/capa.12175.

Wilson, Woodrow. 1887. "The Study of Administration." *Political Science Quarterly* 2, no. 2: 197–222. https://doi.org/10.2307/2139277.

ABOUT THE AUTHORS

Alex Marland is a professor of political science at Memorial University in St. John's and a former public servant in the Government of Newfoundland and Labrador. Alex's interest in the practical side of governance is grounded in his discreet research interviews with politicians, political staff, and public servants. His book *Brand Command: Canadian Politics and Democracy in the Age of Message Control* (UBC Press 2016) won the Donner Prize for Best Public Policy Book by a Canadian.

Jared J. Wesley is a pracademic—a practicing political scientist and former public servant—whose career path to the University of Alberta's Department of Political Science has included senior management positions in the Alberta Public Service (APS). While in Alberta's Executive Council Office, he gained valuable experience in the development of public policy and intergovernmental strategy. He also served as Director of Learning and Development in the Alberta Public Service Commission, establishing policies and curriculum to train public servants at all levels of the APS. As an Associate Professor of Political Science, he studies and teaches the politics of bureaucracy and the bureaucracy of politics.

INDEX